Twilight Dwellers

GHOSTS
GHOULS
& GOBLINS

Twilight Dwellers

OF COLORADO

MaryJoy Martin

PRUETT PUBLISHING COMPANY

Boulder, Colorado

First Edition

    4 5 6 7 8 9

Printed in the United States of America

Library of Congress Cataloging in Publication Data

Martin, MaryJoy, 1955-
  Twilight dwellers.

  Bibliography: p.
  1. Ghosts—Colorado.   I. Title.
BF1472.U6M37 1985   133.1'09788   85-16716
ISBN 0-87108-686-7 (pbk.)

Book and cover design by Bob Schram

To my parents,
Kim,
and Sir George Wade
with love . . .
and in memory of R.G. "Pete" Gones

CONTENTS

PREFACE

rom haunted cemeteries to demon-infested mountains, from will-o'-the-wisps to impalpable presences, Colorado has had and still has enough ghosts, gases, and goblins to groan, shriek, and belch in the pages of several volumes. Where there have been men, women, children, dogs, and mules, there are the disembodied spirits of men, women, children, dogs, and mules.

Every historical town or ghost of an historical town has its crew of spooks. Lumber camps, farms, ranches, and outhouses are not without them. Even before the white man brought his variety of ghosts to Colorado, the Indian had hundreds of his own to thicken the atmosphere. It would require more than my expected lifespan to put the entire discourteous, lecherous, crude, banging, clanging lot of them in a book, and I have no intention of becoming a ghost-writer. Thus only the more significant ghost sightings and unexplained phenomena seen or originating in Colorado's past appear in this book. This includes those encountered by more than one person, those that have continued to haunt to the present, and those that elicited much attention upon their inception.

Left unmentioned are the endless parade of privately owned modern ghosts and the numerous new ghosts, which, upon investigation, seem to be promotional mischief. These will probably disappear in time. There may be persons who ardently desire to have and to hold a genuine specter of their very own, but a Scotsman once said a house with a *real* ghost is quite impossible to sell and more impossible to live in.

Despite the recent rash of ghost sightings (particularly in Denver), fewer have been seen of late than were seen in Colorado's Victorian past. Perhaps these incorporeal marauders are keeping a low profile, or perhaps there are fewer people who will acknowledge a ghost's presence and report it—in this age of technology that sort of thing indicates a chap is functioning on defective software. But! "Thar's ghosts in them thar hills" yet. There are even some convincing ones for the skeptics. The ghosts have not been put to rest. They have not wearied of their unique talents. They simply need attention, waiting for that special person to whom they might properly present themselves. Spend a night in a particular haunt and see if one pops up. These Victorian ghosts have (and had) more vigor, passion, and intrigue than the dishwater ilk of recent invention, which seem single-mindedly attached to gore and slime.

I hope this book will not only reintroduce the shades of the past and the stories behind them, but will also encourage them to be on speaking terms with the slightly more solid citizens of the present. And vice versa. Whether ghosts are actually the disembodied spirits of the dead, or some sort of visible emotional energy or imprint on time and space in a particular location, or whether they are the result of suggestion or a manifestation of guilt, or whether there is some actual power manipulating the senses, there is no denying ghosts have been seen or experienced throughout the centuries. They have altered history and individual's lives. Ghosts are an indispensable part of Colorado's heritage, and forever they are waiting, watching. Rediscover them.

"They are perfectly harmless," said Mr. James Stoner, a gentleman who had the opportunity to wrestle with a few in 1893. "Perfectly harmless...perfectly harm...less..." he muttered that dark morning. Then he expired.

Montrose, Colorado 31 October 1984
MaryJoy Martin

TWILIGHT DWELLERS

Softly, softly shadows fall,
    whispering mysteries of the past,
        calling, calling to vanished men...
            and the Twilight Dwellers come slipping back.

Out of the night winds they arise,
    out of the dust of forgotten dreams,
        touching the souls of those who linger,
           of those who dare to believe.

INTRODUCTION

Twilight Dwellers

he twilight dwellers, the people of Colorado's past, died longing to be remembered. Some have their names on mountains, on cities, on rivers, and on roads. But most have no more than a name carved on a green-tinted marble stone. Some have less. They have sunk into the earth, dust of dust, left to the night's melancholy song, their names unrecalled. Yet their spirits, or the energy of their having lived, still lingers in the high and awesome places, spirits as awesome as the peaks. They had strength in living and greater strength in dying, never fearful of the vastness of the journey before them.

These were the ordinary people who devoured life with a passion, for life was nearly all they possessed. They were the people who gave Colorado her character, her vigor. They had big dreams, simple dreams, shared dreams, and dreams of their own. They reached for the very sun. Some touched it, some died trying. Now in the quiet places they wait for columbines to bloom again, and their dreams are a faint echo in the cities they left behind—quaint, oddly familiar places like Kit Carson, Julesburg, Cripple Creek, Silver Cliff, Telluride, places clinging to the old songs and fading memories.

The cities nestled on Colorado's bosom invite us to touch their past, to discover the intensity of life that made them bloom, to hear that echo, however faint. Perhaps the sound is more than an echo we hear. Is that teamsters' shouts? Mules braying? Guns ringing? Widows crying? Is that someone there in that sagging, slivery building...a face in that darkened window...no, it is gone. But was someone there? Who can say what lingers in the shadows of these arthritic cities? Who can say what dares to come out of the past, stirring the memories, crying to be heard? Is it merely the wind whispering on soft summer days...or is it *something* more?

Since man was first awed and terrified by the mystery of death, he has believed in spirits and life beyond the grave. The mystery of life itself has produced belief in other spirits and demons that breathe existence into animate and inanimate creation, spirits malignant and benign, to be worshipped, feared, placated, and avoided. Tales of these were passed from father to son, from mother to daughter.

According to ancient Arapaho and Ute legends, Colorado has never been without her own ghosts and goblins. Legends passed from generation to generation speak of supernatural beings cavorting here in the lakes and springs, roaring in the mountain hollows, and dancing with fire and wind long before the Indian made the valleys and plains his home.

When the Spaniards came searching for gold, they brought ghosts and demons with them, adding to the vast horde already present. Then in the blink of a watergod's eye, explorers, trappers, and traders arrived on the scene. Sidling after them was a band of explorer, trapper, and trader ghosts. The explorers and trappers had not only their own phantoms to contend with, but several mentioned coming into contact with the various spirits and demons of Indian and Spanish legend.

Following the trappers came the prospectors, the pioneers, European immigrants, Chinese, Russians, men, women, children, dogs, mules, trains, and marble tombstones. And with them came all their ghosts and goblins.

The pioneer life was harsh. The camps and early mining towns hardly supported civilization. They were often primitive, filthy, dangerous, and at the mercy of cholera, bullets, and lynchers. Death's shadow lurked in every squalid corner, hoarding the invalid masses to her bosom, leaving their corpses in the cold, creeping hours before dawn. These reckless days generated great men and great ghosts; they were the very essence of ghost tradition.

The ghosts and goblins wept and laughed, warned and pleaded, guided and led astray. Many tales of them had European counterparts, tales used to teach children or keep them in line. But the largest class of tales sprang from the turbulence of the territory and the times. It seemed if a man died in a violent way, whether by accident, by his own hand, or by someone else's, he inevitably wound up as a ghost. Very few of Colorado's ghosts belonged to persons who died of natural causes and were buried in peace. Ghost tales flourished when death was at its worst.

The truly absurd ghosts and goblins, not necessarily the result of someone's demise, were blamed on the Irish (or their whiskey) and the Cornish. Wherever Cornish folk were there were little "Tommy-knockers who dwelt in the dark mines." The more Cornish miners in an area, the more Tommyknockers abounded, along with all the other supernatural creatures the people of Cornwall were accustomed to dragging about. Central City had a very large Cornish population and, not unexpectedly, a very large Tommyknocker, ghost, and goblin population. Instead of calling herself the "richest square mile on earth," the city could have easily called herself the "hauntedest square mile on earth."

Cripple Creek and Leadville also had an enormous ghost citizenry, but not due to the Cornish. In all likelihood it was because these two cities were among those with the most violence in their history. Their cemeteries boasted so many ghosts that a man once saw a ghost funeral procession in the Cripple Creek cemetery, complete with a brass band and spectral hearse.

Cemetery ghosts drifting about the weedy graves and iron-fenced plots were among the commonest. They were part of tradition: the murder victim restless till avenged, the person improperly buried, the lynched man with the rope still around his shadowy neck, and the tragically lonesome little child. What better place for a spook than a cemetery? Such ghosts were expected and accepted, if not encouraged.

The unexpected ghosts that popped up at lawn parties, shrieked in chimneys, stole shaving mugs, and tossed furniture about were the most dreaded. At the same time, they enjoyed the most attention.

Ghosts of early Colorado, from the time of the Indian through the first pioneers who altered forever this land and its spectral population, enjoyed undisturbed popularity. Few questioned the authenticity of apparitions; the spirits were simply there, "take 'em or leave 'em." No one chased them down to see what sort of material they were made from. No one called in the local medium to put them to rest.

The pioneers actually had little time for analyzing spooks, but they did have time to notice them. Ghost sightings gradually increased from the 1840s, peaking in the mid-1870s. These included apparitions of every sort: poltergeists, wraiths, fetches, phantom coaches, trains, and critters, and a goblin hither and thither. Their great numbers prompted the editors of the *Rocky Mountain News* on 14 November 1874 to write: "The *News* hereby declares its purpose to insert gratuitously notices of no more ghosts. They are becoming altogether too common, and the denizens of the other world appear to be encouraged by the attention they receive in this, to make unduly frequent visits." That hardly quelled their activity, but there was a decline in reported sightings from 1879 through the first half of the 1880s. Then spiritualism revived the lagging spirits.

Self-proclaimed spiritualists and seances had been parlor entertainment since the Fox Sisters, Kate, Leah, and Margaretta, had commenced their "table-rapping" in 1847 in Arcadia, New York. In the late 1880s spiritualism was reborn with a fury in Colorado's larger cities, with the most intense activity centered in Denver, Colorado Springs, Manitou Springs, and Leadville. It became a fashion. It became a pseudoscience. Clairvoyants, mediums, and psychical research societies sprang up like mushrooms after heavy rains, conducting experiments to explore and decipher the spirit world.

Ghosts were explained...and explained away. They were invoked, brought forth on command, instructed, and consulted. Through mediums they uncovered crimes and exposed criminals. Experts in the field classified the phantoms, determined their behavior patterns and proper habitat, and declared those who failed to fit their specifications impostors and frauds. Ghosts were photographed, examined, numbered, bagged, and bottled. Eventually the exploitability of ghostchasing and seances went the way of vapor and gas. Not so with ghosts.

Ghosts continued to appear in Colorado in the decades of the 1920s, 1930s, and 1940s, with major displays of spectral terror and nonsense throughout the state. Their grandest exhibit of this era was in 1946 in Aguilar, a small town in southern Colorado. For nearly a month the town was in the grip of a frightening creature described as a phantom. Although the thing departed, that doesn't mean it won't be back.

Colorado refuses to give up her ghosts. The numerous spooks reported in the Victorian days are still knocking about. They seem to beckon from untenanted houses, cemeteries, abandoned railroads, and mines. One might be seen waiting on the porch of a forlorn house just as twilight falls, dressed in satin of silver-blue, diamonds encircling her neck. Then she is gone.

Softly evening comes, calling to the twilight dwellers to dance their dance, to sing their songs, to linger until the light of dawn.

CHAPTER I

Buried in Haste

horse and rider, formed of transparent shadow and light, skirted the restless grasses, fleet-hooved and soundless. The rider urged his beast on into the air, where they became sunlit wind.

Staring in awe and fear at the hill where the phantom rider disappeared, Lester Lovell whispered to his brother, Griffin, that he was sure the thing they had just seen was the ghost of John Fagan. Lester thought it best to get out of the area as soon as possible. Every tale he had heard concerning Fagan's ghost was unpleasant.

His brother had other ideas. Griffin suggested they should try to capture the ghost for exhibition and thereby make their fortune. Believing they were near John Fagan's grave, Griffin said all they need do was find the grave and wait there until the phantom returned to it.

Lester tried to make Griffin be reasonable and continue on to Colorado City, but Griffin finally convinced him the scheme was possible. Reluctantly Lester agreed to help find the grave.

With the courage of lions the brothers rode into a dense stand of pines crowning the hill before them. They searched the area in circles until, just at sunset, they found an arrangement of rocks suggestive of the forty-year-old grave they sought. Here they made camp to await the ghost of John Fagan.

In 1832 John Fagan was among a company of volunteer soldiers from Bent's Old Fort who were commissioned to protect travelers from Indian raiders along the Santa Fe Trail. With a half dozen men, Fagan was scouting north of the fort along the base of the Rocky Mountains. Rumor had established an unfriendly Arapaho band somewhere near the headwaters of Cherry Creek.

One wintry afternoon the soldiers detected tracks in the snow leading into a small valley between two forested hills. As the company was noisy and awkward with their horses and supply mules, John Fagan was volunteered to scout ahead.

By evening a violent northwest wind was roaring off the mountains,

driving heavy snows before it. John Fagan had not returned. The
other soldiers waited out the storm encamped beneath an overhanging
rock ledge. The storm raged through the night and the next day. The
afternoon of the third day the wind had died, and pale sunlight
squeezed through the gray clouds.

The soldiers went in search of their missing comrade. Fagan's horse
was discovered with a stiff upper lip and a stiffer lower shank in a
snow drift. Nearby, wrapped in his bedroll and curled up by a snow-
smothered fire, was John Fagan. He was as stiff as his horse, if not
stiffer.

Before they had a chance to feel sorry for their scout, the soldiers
heard bizarre birdcalls in the distant trees. A call sounded from the
hill opposite them. Another answered it. A flock of Kentucky
Warblers may have been blown off course, but the soldiers had
doubts. Offering their apologies, the men hastily buried John Fagan,
bedroll and all, beneath a pile of rocks. They hurried away from the
lonely grave near the headwaters of Cherry Creek.

When they had traveled several miles and felt safe from an Indian
attack, the soldiers' thoughts turned to Fagan. Certainly he had appeared dead enough to require burial, but were they sure? Had they
checked his vital signs? Perhaps he really wasn't dead, and maybe they
could have revived him if they had only tried. A dreadful mistake!
They convinced themselves the unfortunate scout was buried alive,
but recalling the warblers, knew it was best to continue their south-
ward journey. Ah, miserable moment! Every step of the way the men
fretted in their hearts over the fate of John Fagan.

Back at Bent's Fort the soldiers confessed their terrible sin, saying
surely Fagan's spirit would rise up and haunt them. Before spring
came there was word that Fagan had done exactly that. Tales of John
Fagan's ghost riding the windswept prairie had in a short time reached
as far south as Santa Fe and as far east as Chouteau's Landing in
Missouri.

Day or night the spirit was glimpsed on his wild rides. His horse's
hooves never touched the grass. He rarely made a sound. He terrorized the vast plain, riding through traders' camps, scattering cattle
herds, flying out of the wind to vanish before awed eyes. Trappers,
hunters, soldiers, and Indians saw the ghost. Niwot of the Arapahoes
even saw the disembodied spirit of John Fagan and shot at the ethereal scout, but he missed his mark. The spirit laughed defiantly as he
rode into the sunlight. The ghost was seen as far north as Fort Lupton
and as far south as Bent's Fort. Most of the time he preferred to

haunt his burial site, which was near the crest of a gently sloping, pine-covered hill, about fifty miles south of Denver, where Cherry Creek's limpid streams sprang from the earth.

By the summer of 1873, when the Lovell brothers were inspired to capture John Fagan, the ghost and tales of him were quite popular throughout the territory. Many a man and woman were victimized by the spook. Many a horse balked when he was near. This was the Lovells' chance for fame and fortune if they could bring the spirit to Denver and exhibit him, perhaps as circus men exhibit bewhiskered ladies.

At best, Griffin and Lester Lovell were entrepreneurs. At worst, they were common rustlers. Having spent many years gophering in the hills for gold and being soundly disappointed, the brothers had turned to slouching about the territory taking odd jobs here and there waiting for opportunity to present itself. John Fagan's spirit presented himself instead.

The wind was mournfully blowing over Fagan's grave while Griffin and Lester stared beyond the brightness of the fire into the deep darkness. The beyond was made all the darker for the two men squatting close enough to the fire to fry their eyelids. They had not yet devised a means of catching the spirit. As night firmly settled on them, they were unsure of their willingness to even try. Finally they drifted into sleep.

They were jolted awake when one of their horses frantically trampled over their camp, whining and snorting. Griffin grabbed his rifle. Lester grabbed Griffin. They strained to hear Whatever was there in the woods.

At that moment out of the darkness flew the softly luminous form of John Fagan on his steed. He crashed through the trees, through the smoldering campfire, over Lester (who fainted away), and on over the hill's crest. Instantly he returned, his horse's hooves stamping to cinders the fire and kicking up dirt, pine needles, and grass. Then all was darkness and dread.

Griffin had been struck speechless, but regained his composure by degrees. He crept over to his brother. Lester required several pints of water in his face before he responded to Griffin. When he was finally aroused, the two fled to Colorado City, riding the night through. Never again were they hampered by the desire to catch a ghost. They may have even become honest men.

John Fagan continued his incorporeal career. He favored no one and never exhibited friendly qualities. At a settlement called Spring

Valley, near Fagan's burial place, the ghost rider ripped through a lady's laundry and scattered linens, longjohns, and petticoats about the hills. At Kuhn's Crossing and Hugo he performed similar favors with line-drying clothes. In Suffolk, east of Colorado Springs, John Fagan took an unwilling gentleman for a wild night ride. Only a few hours before, the man had been scolded by his wife for repeated bouts of drunkenness. After the ride he was said to have miraculously reformed. Once the ghost was seen skirting the track in the path of a locomotive on the Atchison, Topeka & Santa Fe Railroad, keeping his horse at a steady pace before the astounded engineer. In Elbert County a large herd of cattle was stampeded by the unscrupulous wraith, who turned from this accomplishment to ride circles around the rancher's daughter. He was also the cause of Matt Riddelberger's misfortune.

Matt and his friend, Zan Hickland, were on a return trip to Huerfano County from Denver, where Matt had purchased a prized white mule. The men were traveling in a buckboard wagon, camping beneath it at night. They had a pothouse supply of whiskey with them, which they ungrudgingly swilled. By the time both had consumed enough to embalm half the population of Philadelphia, the sun had set. Near Fagan's grave they decided to camp.

The men knew the story of John Fagan, yet in their state of advanced placidity would not have feared a score of spirits. After they ate their supper, they went to sleep.

Late into the snoring and snorting Matt awoke and nudged Zan with his elbow.

"Pard," said Matt, "I see a ghost."

"Oh, go to sleep, Matt," came a drowsy reply. "There hain't no ghost round here."

"But I see a ghost."

Finally Matt determined that the ghost had left, so he went back to sleep. Just before dawn he awoke.

The gray sky had not yet shed its stars in the west, where sky and morning mist seemed to fold into one gossamer cloak from heavens to woodlands. In the east a faint streak of gold hinted at sunshine. Matt stretched his arms and shook the dew from his hair.

"Pard!" he said, poking Zan. "There's a ghost!"

Zan crawled out of the blankets to see the ghost. He let out a sound like a disturbed toad, grabbed his rifle, and blazed away at the misty form. It dropped to the ground.

"Ha!" said Zan. "Ol' Chief Left Hand may miss, but when I shoot a ghost, I fetch him."

The two men rushed to the still-writhing figure. Matt, raising his hands, cried out in horror.

"Damn it, Zan! You've shot my white mule!"

They heard laughing all around them in the misty forest. Then out of the trees rode John Fagan, dashing over the dead mule and off into the awakening dawn.

CHAPTER II

The Headless Highwayman

hot through the heart, William Bruce was found dead at his sawmill on Hardscrabble Creek in Fremont County. Within days, the axed corpse of old William Harkins was discovered at his sawmill on Little Fountain Creek in El Paso County. More appalling discoveries followed: the slain Mr. Addleman at his ranch near Colorado City, the butchered Mr. Binckley and a brother of Colonel George L. Shoup in the Red Hills of South Park, Frank Carter at Cottage Grove near Buckskin, Mr. Lehman and Mr. Seyga of California Gulch murdered in the Red Hills, two unknown slain travelers on the South Park road to Canon City, and the mutilated body of Mr. Petersen on the Currant Creek road near Bumback Springs.

As the list of butchered men grew in that spring of 1863, rage and panic clutched the citizens of the South Park region. Family men barricaded their wives and children in their houses. Others feared to travel upon the roads by day or night. No one knew what horrible brute had descended upon the Park, for there were no witnesses, no clues.

In early May of 1863 a Mr. Chapin was found bleeding to death in the roadside weeds some miles south of Fairplay. He indicated that his assailants numbered two, but slipped into unconsciousness before he could say more. He died the following morning.

A few days later, a freighter was hauling a wagon of lumber from the Buckskin Joe area to Fairplay when he was fired upon from a thicket. The bullet struck him in the chest, but, according to Frank Hall, "was stopped from entering his body by a copy of Lincoln's Emancipation Proclamation and a memorandum book" in his pocket. Quickly turning to see who fired the shot, the freighter spied two Mexicans. As the Mexicans raised their guns to fire again, the freighter lashed his already affrighted ox team into a run never since equalled by those beasts. In Fairplay the freighter related his brush with the assassins, and immediately a search party was organized. Rumor spread that the two Mexicans were the notorious, heartless Espinosa brothers who had come from Chihuahua, murdering two merchants in

Santa Fe and a soldier at Conejos on their northward journey.

A party of seventeen volunteers, with Captain John McCannon as their leader, scouted South Park for many days and nights and at length hit upon a trail near Thirtynine Mile Mountain. Following the trail along Four Mile, or West Oil, Creek into a narrow canyon of weird and grotesque rock outcrops, they traveled up High Creek to a small grassy meadow about twenty miles north of Canon City. There they found the Mexicans' two horses, one of which was hobbled.

Captain McCannon sent four of his men, Billy Youngh among them, to skirt around to the far side of the bandits' camp. Then they all quietly awaited the Espinosas, anxious for vengence.

"In a short time," related Captain McCannon, "the largest of the Espinosas came out of the willows and commenced taking off the hobbles that held his horse. Joseph Lamb fired, the ball breaking the second rib on the right side of Espinosa and passing directly through, broke the second rib on the left side. Sanger fired next, with buckshot, but the horse stumbling over the desperado received the charge. Espinosa raised up on his elbow and commenced firing at me, as I had left my position to look after the other one, supposing that Lamb's and Sanger's firing had done the work. Charles Carter [a brother of one of the Espinosas' victims] then fired, the ball striking Espinosa between the eyes and ranging back, killed him instantly. The other one came in sight, but got off without a shot, through a mistake. I had my gun leveled on him when Julius Sanger cried out, 'For God's sake don't kill Billy Youngh!' They were about the same size and were dressed alike. I dropped my gun to get a better look, and he [the Espinosa] seeing the motion, threw himself over into the ravine and was seen no more."

A search of the bandits' camp turned up the bloodstained clothing of at least a dozen slain men, along with stolen money, pocketbooks, watches, rings, bracelets, and other trinkets, a large butcher knife, an ax, and a pair of boots belonging to a dead gentleman in the San Luis Valley. On the dead Espinosa's body was a prayer book and a list of thirty-two murdered men's names. In the prayer book were many mad religious ramblings penned by the dead man, one ending thus: "The Virgin Mary will be sitting on my head until I die in her arms, amen Jesus!"

Although the South Park residents felt relieved the elder Espinosa's career was ended, they feared the other would continue in the bloody family business. The governor and relatives of several of the slain men offered rewards totaling $1500 for the life of the remaining brother.

The younger Espinosa had escaped to New Mexico, where he recruited his nephew, a boy of fifteen. The two returned to Colorado, making camp in the region of Grayback Gulch and Sangre de Cristo Pass. Along roads of that area, the San Luis Valley and South Park, the two carried out murders and robberies and rustling, but for only a few months.

Tom Tobins, a resident of the San Luis Valley and a sturdy mountaineer, knew the territory better than the deer that lived in it. With the $1500 reward in mind and an inflexible desire to end the murders, Tobins, in company with a few Fort Garland soldiers, went in search of the highwaymen. A thin spiral of smoke and ravens circling above a thicket told the mountaineer he had located his prey. He slipped noiselessly on his hands and knees through the underbrush until he was in a position to take certain aim. He shot and killed both Espinosas and to prove the fact, removed the head of the elder and brought it to Fort Garland, leaving the corpses to hungry ravens.

It took the Colorado General Assembly thirty years to come up with Tom Tobins's reward money; meanwhile the infamous head remained at Fort Garland in the possession of Dr. Waggoner, post physician, who preserved it in alcohol. When Dr. Waggoner left the service he took the head with him. While traveling over Sangre de Cristo Pass on his way to Pueblo, the doctor's wagon was upset, jolting out several of his possessions. The jar the bandit's head was in broke, and the head went bumping down the roadside. Dr. Waggoner retrieved it, took it to Pueblo, buried it, and later disinterred it to clear the flesh and preserve the skull.

A peculiar practice of the day among physicians and men of science was to keep the skulls of violent criminals with a vague notion of discovering the source of their violence. Some gentlemen had marvelous collections of these grisly trophies, one being Professor Denton and another being Professor Fowler, who boasted the skulls of Messrs. Griswold, Musgrave, Franklin, Myers, and Dugan, all criminals of early Denver. When Professor Fowler learned Espinosa's skull was held by Dr. Waggoner, he prevailed on the physician to turn it over to him.

Meanwhile, the ghost of the decapitated bandit was none too pleased with the disappearance of his topmost portion and went on a rampage. As early as 1865, people reported seeing Espinosa's ghost madly riding a black horse in search of his missing head. He especially haunted the Sangre de Cristo Pass area (immediately north of North La Veta Pass), but also terrorized the San Luis Valley and South Park.

At the close of a summer day in 1869, Charles Streeter was returning home to San Luis after a freight delivery in Placer, a new mining camp north of Fort Garland on the Sangre de Cristo road. The wagon wheels were spinning up golden clouds of dust in the last light of day as Streeter stampeded his mule team south, counting on a tall whiskey at journey's end.

Still several miles from San Luis when dusk fell on the valley, Streeter noticed an unmoving horse and rider blocking the road ahead of him. The teamster hauled back on the reins, bellowed at his beloved, cussed mules, and came to a perfect stop in front of the bold equestrian.

The stranger, dressed in dark clothing, blended like a shadow into the dark color of his horse. Pointing a gun at Streeter, he put out his hand, silently demanding the teamster's money.

Streeter's initial annoyance turned into a chuckle and then a loud guffaw. He slapped his hand on his thigh and roared with laughter.

"Just try and shoot me!" snorted Charles Streeter. "I'll bet you couldn't shoot the broad side of Arapahoe County!"

He cracked leather over his mules' ears and went on toward San Luis, laughing till the tears ran down his cheeks. Streeter feared few things in life, and a lone bandit wasn't among them, especially a lone bandit minus his head. A man without his head, reasoned the teamster, would find it exceedingly difficult to take aim with a gun—one needed eyesight for that operation, and a bandit without a head was also without eyes. He did have one advantage over other bandits, considered Streeter as he chortled into San Luis: without a head and consequently without a face, the desperado needed no disguising mask. Charles Streeter never tired of telling of his encounter with the headless phantom, laughing himself off his chair every time.

Others were less amused by the ghost, especially the superstitious farm and ranch hands in the area. Two young men, Ramon Costa and Juan Sales, nearly got themselves killed in 1874 by leaping down a steep ravine in a desperate attempt to escape the phantom. The men were located the next day, screaming for help. Both sustained broken bones and a terrible fear of highwaymen.

The following year Lieutenant Wilson T. Hartz, quartermaster at Fort Garland, met the headless equestrian on his way from Placer to the military post. The phantom sprang out of nowhere after dark when Lieutenant Hartz was about a mile from Placer. The officer, usually unperturbed by things that breathed down his neck in the night, was nominally upset by the spook. It pursued him in a mad chase all the way to the fort, where Hartz was found to be visibly shaken and his horse spattered with froth and sweat.

"Merely a small inconvenience upon the road," he reported to Lieutenant Colonel Kautz.

During the autumn of that same year, two gentlemen, Phillip McKay, who was a Denver businessman, and his English friend, Thomas Hatchwood, were traveling on horseback up the South Oak Creek road from Huerfano Canyon. As they crossed the mountains at Sangre de Cristo Pass, the headless highwayman reared up in front of them. Hatchwood demanded the phantom's immediate departure in the name of the bishop of Canterbury, but quickly lost his bravado, for headless things had always "made a mouse" of him.

The two men spurred their horses down the mountain and into the trees of Pass Creek with the ghost in pursuit. Reaching the Pass Creek road, they drove hard the next eight miles to the settlement of Malachite. When they glanced back, no highwayman, headless or otherwise, was in sight, but to make certain they had no further disagreeable encounters, McKay and Hatchwood traveled to the San Luis Valley via Mosca Pass.

In July 1879 a man named Joe Williamson was camping alone on a tributary of Currant Creek in South Park. He was awakened one night by a horse thrashing through his camp and was very nearly trampled by the beast. Williamson described the horse as huge and black, its saddle of the Spanish type.

"I had often scoffed at the tales of a specter," said Williamson, "which was claimed to range the South Park, until that night. The rider was thin and small and he had no head on his shoulders. This vision alone could strike terror in the strongest of men, but the horse and rider came upon me, the horse lashing the air with its hooves. I feared my death was imminent. The fiend struck me a terrible blow upon the left temple with his gun and I stumbled. I do not pretend to have escaped death under my own power, yet when I next awoke it was morning and I was alive. I was several yards from my camp, in the muddy creek, none the worse for wear."

Williamson departed South Park in haste, vowing to never grant the phantom a second opportunity at knocking his head about.

The ghost continued its depraved career, terrorizing, attacking, and pursuing residents and travelers through South Park and the San Luis Valley. He also continued to look for his missing head, but because Professor Fowler had spirited it away to places unknown, Espinosa would haunt forever.

CHAPTER III

Dead Man's Canyon

o sound but the gentle burbling of Little Fountain Creek and an occasional trilling whistle of a wren broke the uncanny stillness of yellow-eyed dusk. The sun had just sunk behind Blue Mountain, leaving a saffron sky and purple shadows as J.P. Galloway rode toward Colorado Springs, which lay ten miles north. Apprehensive, Galloway felt compelled to glance frequently over his shoulder. He disliked riding after dark through Dead Man's Canyon. Something always seemed to be lurking there.

Below a jutting red rock cliff hemmed by a dense thicket of scrub oak, Galloway's horse balked. The animal refused to set another hoof forward. Scanning the cedar, juniper, and pine forest on the ridge, Galloway discerned no sign of lurkers. He stared hard at the golden cottonwoods along Little Fountain Creek, wondering if the ghostly humps of seeding clematis and red Virginia creeper slung high in the trees were actually the lurkers his eye sought. The horse knew something was near. J.P. Galloway shuddered. Because he could see no person or dreaded thing awaiting him, his fear only increased. Where was it? When would it spring out of hiding? Would he die this night?

As the purple shadows deepened, the sweet scent of autumn leaves and dusty grass wafted on the cool air. A dry rustling sound disturbed the thicket behind Galloway. He strapped his horse's flank, terrified, frenzied. The horse bolted, pitching its rider into the creek. Scrambling to his feet, J.P. Galloway saw the thing he dreaded. White, transparent, the form of a bearded man was coming toward him. The apparition flew soundlessly through the thicket, over the bushes, and straight at Galloway, an ax embedded in its skull. Galloway shot at it with his revolver, but onward it came, laughing hideously. The apparition flew over or through or under the man, he was uncertain which, for at that moment he fled, forgetting the rheumatism in his hip, forgetting the water in his boots, forgetting his fine new hat in the creek. He didn't forget how to scream.

Lawrence Poole and Adam T. Baker, traveling in the same direction as

Galloway, hurried to the screaming man's assistance. Seeing the phantom in pursuit of J.P. Galloway and mistaking it for a remarkably agile highwayman with peculiar head adornment, Poole immediately seized his rifle and shot at the thing while Baker dismounted and shot at it with his pistol.

The phantom dived at Galloway like a crazed hawk, knocked him into some rocks, and turned on the two other men, laughing loudly at their bullets as it sprang all around them. Confusion and wild shooting ensued. When the phantom finally departed into the thicket, Lawrence Poole discovered he had shot his horse in the ear, and Adam Baker discovered he had shot himself in the toes. Galloway, dizzy and shaking, crawled out of the rocks, thanked the men for their help, and passed into unconsciousness at their feet.

Later that night in Colorado Springs, J.P. Galloway kept babbling about being attacked by "old Harkins's ghost." The doctor tending him blamed the babbling and ghost on Galloway's head injury, but when he heard the same tale from Poole and Baker, he could contrive no excuse. However, the doctor was suspicious of Baker's mental stability, since that gentleman had succeeded in shooting himself in the foot when "Harkins's ghost" swooped upon him. Perhaps Harkins had a very short ghost?

That late autumn night in 1874 marked the eleventh year the ghost of William Harkins had haunted Dead Man's Canyon. The red rock area along Little Fountain Creek had been named for Harkins posthumously. While the old man lived in the canyon and operated a sawmill there no one bothered to call the place "Harkins Canyon." It gained its name not so much in honor of the man, but in honor of his remains. He was found axed to death in the spring of 1863, his body left a few feet from the cabin with the ax buried in his forehead. It was generally believed that a band of Mexican religious fanatics committed the atrocious crime, stole Harkins's white work horse, and robbed his cabin. The murder was avenged, but Harkins's ghost clung to Dead Man's Canyon, sometimes haunting alone, sometimes in partnership with a white ghost horse, and always behaving obnoxiously and antagonistically. Certainly a ghost with an ax in its head had a good reason to be ill-tempered.

J.P. Galloway's headache, from the ghost knocking his head on the rocks, was eventually relieved, but he swore he would never again ride through Dead Man's Canyon. He would go by the Crooked Canyon road even if it meant going several miles out of his way. Other people were not so timid.

In July 1884 Mrs. Clark Wyatt and her small grandson were driving through Dead Man's Canyon one afternoon in a one-horse buggy. Mrs. Wyatt was taking the child to the settlement of Turkey Creek, a few miles south of the canyon, where his parents lived. As the travelers stopped to pick a bouquet of roadside flowers for the boy's mother, William Harkins's shade sprang out of the scrub oak and frightened the youngster to tears.

"Shame on you!" said Mrs. Wyatt to the ghost. She struck him in the ear with the quirt. "If you dare bother me when I return this evening, I'll whip you more than once, I will. Scaring a baby, shame!"

When Mrs. Wyatt returned later to Colorado Springs, the ghost made no appearance. A grandmother's lash had succeeded where bullets failed.

Many a muleskinner and bullwhacker told tales of being pursued by the phantom in Dead Man's Canyon, especially in the 1860s and 1870s. The haunted area was part of the Cheyenne Mountain road between Colorado Springs and Canon City. Some freighters were annoyed by the ghost for twenty miles, while others were only attacked in the canyon. A few of them collected more than Mr. Harkins's vengeful spirit, for they reported being chased by a phantom horse or a pair of phantom horses, riderless but bearing phantom saddles. One man was besieged by a half dozen phantom women (which may have had nothing to do with Dead Man's Canyon, but something to do with the freighter's conscience), and a Captain Marshall P. Felch saw a phantom horse, rider, and dog in the canyon.

A young lady, Gertrude Osborn, had asked Captain Felch and his wife to find the lady's sweetheart, who had traveled to the California Gulch gold fields. For a year Miss Osborn and the young man, Oliver Kimball, had corresponded. Then his letters suddenly ceased to arrive, leading Miss Osborn to believe he had been dealt with foully. Since she lived in the East but knew the captain and his wife, living in Denver, she wrote to them, enlisting their help.

Captain Felch had no success in finding Kimball in California Gulch. He only learned the name of a possible mining partner, Dave Griffin. In September 1867, while the captain was in Canon City, he received a letter from his wife that said Gertrude was at their Denver home; would he please return at once. The wife related in her letter that in nightmares the young lady saw her beloved in a terrible struggle with a man who stabbed and slashed him. She described the scene in minute detail. Captain Felch recognized it as Dead Man's Canyon. But Gertrude also said she sensed she would die as soon as Oliver

Kimball's body was discovered.

Setting out straightaway from Canon City, Marshall Felch was caught in a storm. He waited till it stopped before continuing, but this caused him to arrive in Dead Man's Canyon after dark, a convenient hour to be bothered by specters. He smelled something faintly similar to the odor of rotting flesh.

"Do not imagine that this occasioned me any nervousness," related the captain. "I had too lately been in the army and slept among the dead to feel any timidity."

Shortly he saw a phantom horse pass him and went after it, coming to a dilapidated cabin, where the horse stopped. A phantom dog followed a phantom miner out of the cabin. The miner mounted the horse and rode up the canyon, the ghost dog and Captain Felch following. In an area of fallen rock, Marshall Felch saw a vision of the phantom man in a struggle. The man was struck down with a dagger and vanished. The dog and horse also vanished.

In the morning Captain Felch and the son of a nearby rancher returned to the place of the vision. They dug up the body of Oliver Kimball, who was wearing an identifying bracelet. The dagger was still in his breast. On the dagger's blade were the letters "D.G."

When Captain Felch reached Denver, his wife informed him Gertrude had died the previous night, muttering that her "darling was found at last," and she was going to him. Later the captain went to California Gulch to tell Dave Griffin of the discovered murdered man. Griffin went into his cabin and shot himself dead, according to Fitz Mac, who wrote the ghost story for a Denver newspaper in the 1880s.

Marshall Felch was the only person to ever see the ghosts of Oliver Kimball, his horse, and his dog in Dead Man's Canyon. The red rock canyon belonged to William Harkins's ghost. Unlike Kimball, Harkins was durable and determined never to leave off his haunting sport.

The Cheyenne Mountain road is now the paved Highway 115 to Canon City. Although William Harkins's cabin and sawmill have long since decayed into the tall grasses, the red cliff face, scrub oak thickets, cottonwood trees, and Little Fountain Creek of Dead Man's Canyon have seen no great change since 1863. It is not always the eerie hoot of a Great Horned Owl one hears nor the luminous eyes of a coyote one suddenly sees in the thickets. Sometimes the voice and eyes belong to a phantom—a phantom with an ax in his forehead. Beware his ill-temper; he has had an enormous headache for more than a century.

Tipis Out of the Mist

My heart is heavy within me
like crushed and broken raven's wings.
I cannot fly,
for my soul's wings are in sorrow,
sorrowing beneath a bent world.
My people are scattered,
feeding the thirsty dust with their blood.
Oh God! Oh Great God!
I see so much restlessness
in their crying souls.
They try to hide it in laughter,
but in silent moments it steals to their lips,
and they look like the dead,
a fleeting life within;
like the dead not dead,
they no longer recall the freedom in the wind.
Oh God! Oh Great God!
Touch the earth with your ancient song,
give us a glimmer of starlight!

CHAPTER IV

Tipis Out of the Mist

 rairie silence is unbroken in the cold November hours of waning night; no bird calls in the frosty air. The sky is moonless, blackrobed, and stars are too distant to weave their ancient songs into the human tapestry. Creeping dawn light tempts the shadows out of the mist. Yet shadows form on the bleeding breast of the plains.

Shadows, dark yet luminous, visible yet like water, shadows not cast by light but formed from the November mist. Flowing out of the earth, they rise from the ragged vegetation along Big Sandy Creek. They are women, as beautiful as the running deer, stirring the ash of fire pits. They are noble men wrapped in blankets with feathers in their hair. There is peaceful smoke rising out of the tipis. There is a distant sound like a great many buffalo. A child stares into the morning, betrayed, knowing suddenly it is not the buffalo she hears. Then the child, the men, the women, the tipis sink into the grass like the frost as sunlight vanquishes night's shadows, leaving only a song and a dry creek bed.

The song, low and solemn, is hidden among the cottonwood trees. It is so broken with anguish that the human ear cannot listen, the human heart cannot bear it. Black as raven feathers, the song tangles the air in pleading notes till it rises in a wail of profound grief; then falls again to an utter quiet, a forgiving quiet, yet never forgetting the pain. Softly touching the soul, gliding like the plaintive trill of a bird, the song is lost in the vastness of the prairie.

Big Sandy Creek is lifeless most of the year, dry eternal sands without a voice. Each spring the rains come and the music of rushing water delights sleeping roots of cottonwoods, thistle, and stubborn grass with arpeggios of flute and harp. The bluffs above the creek, where once Indian ponies grazed, burst into green for one brief magnificent moment, an antiphon for the killdeer and hawk, pronghorn and mouse, owl and snake. Yet fleeting the music, fleeting the feathered breasts, fleeting the life as summer gathers the color of green into yellow, and the full cottonwoods nod in warm wind and white sun.

Sheltered in these cottonwoods at the edge of the creek, at the edge of eternity, where the Big Sandy bends like a lazy snake, is a holy place touched with sorrow. Men with peaceful hearts once brought their Cheyenne and Arapaho families here to raise their tipis, to wait for spring. White Antelope, One Eye, Left Hand, Black Kettle, and War Bonnet led their people to this spot in the autumn of 1864, believing in the honesty and honor of the white chiefs in Denver and Fort Lyon. They did not know the treachery and hatred that seethed in many of the white men's hearts. They did not know that Colonel John M. Chivington was convinced his God gave him a sacred command to kill the Cheyenne and Arapaho people, any and all wherever they were found. What unholy demongod did the colonel listen to in the dark hours of night? Surely not the Great God, giver of wild game and ripe berries, who splashed the good earth with rain and sun and wind. Surely the Great God had not spoken to Colonel Chivington.

In the stealth of a frosty November night, Colonel Chivington with his Colorado Volunteers, Major Scott Anthony of Fort Lyon and his troops, Lieutenant Wilson and Colonel Shoup with their men, converged upon the sleeping village of Cheyennes and Arapahoes. As dawn broke, the soldiers descended upon the poorly armed people with horses, guns, and howitzers. The soldiers were told by Colonel Chivington that no prisoners were to be taken, all were to be destroyed.

Like a flock of crazed crows, black-hearted, ravenous, the soldiers slaughtered men, women, and children, acting out a nightmare of demon perversity, mutilating, scalping, tearing the hearts, the dignity, the very essence of human spirit and sacredness from the Cheyenne and Arapaho people. A few short hours were filled with long pain and broken life. Black Kettle's proud United States flag flown above his lodge could not protect, could not save. The red stripes became the blood of his children, the white stripes the emptiness of white men's promises, the stars were stars of the dead.

The butchery ended with wailing and moaning. Smoke from dying fires bore the spirits of the dead to their fathers, bore the prayers and anguish to the Great God who wept that day.

Feeling triumphant with only eight of his men dead and several hundred Indians slaughtered, Colonel Chivington and his soldiers claimed souvenirs from the bodies and lodges, hailing their deed as a great victory for the United States government. Victory? Others believed it was clearly murder. Even some at Fort Lyon, Lieutenant

Joseph Cramer and others, felt sick at heart and could not reckon with their part in the massacre, however small.

There was a government investigation into the incident, and Colonel Chivington was cited for court martial but never tried. The sentiment at the time among many frontier settlers was that peace with Indians came only by killing them. The soldiers who had volunteered their services for the single purpose of killing Indians saw the Cheyenne and Arapaho as fiends who slaughtered white men, enslaved white women, and burned, ravaged, and terrorized settlements. Thus affirmed by the feelings of their fellow citizens and the orders of Colonel Chivington, they unleashed their self-righteous vengeance, hatred, and fear upon the Indians.

Yet the infamies of the Sand Creek Massacre could not be ignored or forgotten. Citizens tried to keep the truth of it far away from the heart, for it was painful to face. The Colorado historian, Frank Hall, wrote in 1889, "Whether the battle of Sand Creek was right or wrong, these fiendish acts can never be palliated, nor can there ever be in this world or the next any pardon for the men who were responsible for them. . . . It will not do, as some have done, to fall back to the atrocities of the Indians upon our people as a justification." Memories remained haunted and the chronicles of Colorado bore a bloody stain. Sand Creek would not be forgotten. It could not. Interior human integrity, whisperings of the night owls, and a trick of heaven would never allow the nightmare of 29 November 1864 to fade.

On 2 December 1865 Kipling Brightmaster, a buffalo hunter, reported at Fort Lyon that he had seen a band of Cheyennes encamped in the bend of Big Sandy Creek where Colonel Chivington had engaged in battle the previous year. A scouting party was dispatched to the site but found no sign of Indians having been there. While there they felt a certain dread of the place; one young soldier overcome with sorrow broke down and wept. Returning to Fort Lyon they explained they saw nothing, as was expected. Brightmaster insisted he saw the tipis and Indians. He had not imagined it. He was told to go along his way.

The following November Kipling Brightmaster was again hunting in the massacre area when he saw the same Indian village. Early in the morning he approached the tipis, the frosted grass crunching beneath his horse's hooves. As he drew near, the scene began to fade, until it was obscured by a haze of smoke. He heard a sound as of distant thunder. Then all was still.

Turning his horse and packmules to depart, Brightmaster heard an anguished chant coming from a spot near the cottonwoods. Someone was mourning her dead. He dismounted to investigate, but found no one. The song seemed to be nowhere yet everywhere at once. Brightmaster fled on his horse northward, believing he had encountered Indian ghosts. As he came to the crest of a bluff he glanced behind him. In the morning haze he saw the tipi village in the creek's bow.

Kipling Brightmaster told his tale in Denver. Few wanted to hear it. No one wished to be reminded of the slaughter. They secretly averred that Brightmaster had been alone on the plains far too long. He never returned to the tragic site.

The tipis continued to be seen infrequently by travelers and ranchers, and the unearthly lament heard in the cottonwoods for several decades. The scene was taken to be encamped Indians or a trick of the morning mist, the song ignored as the cry of an injured coyote.

In 1896 two young men witnessed the Cheyenne and Arapaho village with much excitement. They had no doubt they were looking upon a supernatural phenomenon. They saw the tipis again in 1902 and attempted, unsuccessfully, to photograph them. A woman named Mrs. Spencer heard the cry of a child near the place in 1911 and searched several hours, eventually concluding the sound must have been from an animal. Seeking the grave of her pioneer great-grandmother, a New Jersey woman stumbled upon the massacre area in the summer of 1956 and was overwhelmed by grief and terror she could not understand until someone explained what had happened there in 1864. She had felt the secret suffering of the place, not knowing its mystery.

The prairie holds many secrets, ancient secrets whispered by night in the moon-tinted grasses. Secrets of love, of life, of death woven in the solemn blades, touching one another like fingers upon the soul. The prairies have changed yet remain unchanged, singing the same night songs to the owl-moon, a faraway note, singularly sorrowful yet somehow a pleading joy of human life made divine by bloodshed.

When November frost kisses the withered grass, or snow sparkles like a jeweled shroud on the vast plain, the Indian village appears. Faint at the bend in Big Sandy Creek, the tipis stand serene in the early dawn hours. For a moment glory is there, integrity of human character, dignity of human spirit; then only the morning haze and a long ago song that echoes sadly, "I go unto the Far Sky, for only the mountains and the earth last forever."

CHAPTER V

The Effects of Sulfur and High Altitude On the Mental Health of Irish Prospectors

utumn of 1865 found flocks of eager prospectors poking their beaks into ravines and gulches and building shaggy nests on the steep mountains of upper Clear Creek Valley. Silver rumors had lured them this far, and only silver ore would assure they remained.

Word of each new silver discovery filled the Denver newspapers. Argentiferous ores assayed at $200 to $500 per ton created a sensation in the city much like bees preparing to swarm. Silver. Silver! Silver was the resurrection of Francis D. Haverty's miserable soul.

Fresh from Ireland, Francis had become discontented in his native country and hoped America might rekindle those passions lost as a result of his countless failures. Although well educated and of the Irish gentry, Francis had disappointed himself and his family time after time, unable to discover a suitable profession. Now he cast about in a state of devastating purposelessness.

While degenerating in Denver, the tales of the silver El Dorado tugged on some long forgotten cord deep in Francis's heart, stirring within him a desire for adventure in the rugged Rocky Mountains. Up to that moment he had desired very little, except perhaps to pass up no whiskey however poisonous, for whiskey helped him forget his past follies.

Francis D. Haverty was an amiable, courteous, generous gentleman who would never dream of knocking about those monstrous hills alone—adventure was best when shared—and besides, if he did go alone, he was sure to get himself lost. Thus, he planned to organize a prospecting party.

Having dragged his cousin with him from Ireland, Francis informed him of their impending adventure. They were to find a mountain of silver in the remote regions of Clear Creek Valley, fighting the elements, battling fourteen-foot grizzlies, surviving the most treacherous conditions. Ah! Sweet Adventure!

No one knows how the cousin, Caley O' Donnelly, received this exciting news. If he protested, it was to no avail. Caley was a quiet gentleman, a few years younger than Francis. He was devoted to the nuns at a County Waterford convent. How he was devoted is a mystery.

Francis and Caley required more than two to make up a prospecting party, so Francis put word about town of his needs. Shortly, two Irish brothers, Timothy L. and Martin Killeen, joined them, along with Henry Fry, a Pennsylvanian who was unsure of sharing his campfire with that many Irishmen, Jack O'Connell, an ordinary American, and four others.

While Francis knew he wanted to discover silver veins, he did not know how to go about it. The only silver he was familiar with was the tea service and the dinnerware. He also was uncertain how to locate Clear Creek Valley. In short, the party of prospectors needed a guide.

It was their fortune (or perhaps their misfortune) that a faded old prospector, who had been scratching about the territory for decades, was heading in the same direction and offered them his services. This fellow was known as Mad Jack, but his real name was Jack or John or possibly Amos Strong—a surname more descriptive of his odor than his muscle. Mad Jack (who became a ghost later on in Brown Gulch) was thin enough to waltz through a keyhole despite consuming several pounds of flapjacks every morning. This was his only requirement: that the party supply him with enough flour for two months of flapjacks. He had a burro as rusty and as "strong" as himself, and he swore it was part moose. He was not referred to as Mad Jack without reason.

Thus it came to pass in autumn of 1865 that the party of Irishmen and a few assorted Americans set out for the new El Dorado. They were well equipped, Francis Haverty having seen to it that no one lacked necessities, especially himself. He had a morbid dread of scurvy and was sure to include a king's ransom in lemons and limes.

When the prospectors reached upper Clear Creek Valley, Mad Jack led them up one gulch after another, always turning back, telling them his "bur-rah" indicated each gulch was worthless. Mad Jack exhibited great deference toward his fragrant burro, assuring everyone the beast was brilliant in metallurgy. This soon disenchanted the four unnamed members of the party, and they went off on their own. Mad Jack took this as an insult to his and his burro's expertise. He, too, departed, leaving the Irishmen to figure out for themselves how and where to locate their silver seams.

The party pushed on up Clear Creek until Henry Fry suggested they try Kearney Gulch. About a mile up this stream they made camp in a small clearing, and Timothy and Martin Killeen were elected to scare up some meat for the prospectors.

Off into the dense pine and spruce forest Timothy and his brother went, their hearts set on moose meat because of their recent association with Mad Jack, who had praised the flavor of that animal's flesh. Soon Timothy spotted a long brown nose through the trees and pulled the trigger. Henry Fry's pack burro bit the dust. The unfortunate Timothy Killeen was deceived into seeing a burro as a moose—also because of his association with Mad Jack.

Telling himself he was safe among the Irish, Henry Fry forgave Timothy, and they heartily dined on limes and fish.

The following day they went off in pairs to search for signs of silver, Timothy and Martin going together up the west side of Baker Mountain. They became separated. About an hour had elapsed when Martin's screams were heard throughout the forest. Henry, Francis, and Timothy ran to his aid. They found the terrified man tumbling down through the pine needles, his trousers torn and blood on his hands.

"I tell ye! 'Twas a demon, a horrible black demon," he said, coughing on the needles in his mouth.

Martin was taken back to camp, where his wounds were bound. The wounds were nothing serious. They appeared to be claw marks on his legs and hands...claw marks of a demon to be sure.

Henry lost no time searching out the demon for his own satisfaction. He found fresh bear tracks. This he reported to the others.

The unfortunate Martin Killeen was deceived into seeing a bear as a devil. Perhaps.

Meanwhile Jack O'Connell had found what appeared to be silver-bearing surface rock. He dug a bit and brought the ore into camp. Informing his fellow prospectors that he was going to take the ore to Central City to have it assayed, he left them with a few short geology lessons, fearing they were indeed "babes in the woods." On his way down Clear Creek, Jack discovered a more promising lode and never returned to his Irish connection.

Jack's discovery in Kearney Gulch left Francis and his comrades in a delirious state. Silver was there beneath their feet. Silver was on the mountains. Silver was in the creek. Silver was in the tree roots. Their enthusiasm was second only to their lack of knowledge.

That night Colorado did what Colorado has always been fond of doing. She dropped an unexpected eight inches of snow on the party. When they awoke in the morning there was an eerie white silence all about them. Martin was sure it was a sign the devil disapproved of their taking his silver. Caley agreed with him. Surely devils were infesting this entire gulch.

Francis expressed his feeling that life was at last surging through him, knowing he was close to silver with devils to battle. Adventure! He convinced Caley to help him look for silver despite the snow. Henry had already set out to that purpose.

Francis headed up the side of Baker Mountain while Caley followed Kearney Creek toward its source.

Although the sun was shining, Caley noticed the devilish clouds crouching on the peaks of the surrounding mountains. The clouds tumbled and twisted and blossomed into blacker hydras. Coming to a level meadow where the creek flowed gently, Caley saw thin vaporous forms rising from the water. The faint scent of sulfur greeted his nostrils. He approached the creek cautiously, knowing as every good Christian Irishman did that where there was sulfur there quite naturally was the devil.

Standing on the bank, Caley saw the reflections of the snow-laden willow bushes in the water. Then he saw a hideous black face, contorted and bearing horns, just under the surface. It rose up, the long tongue protruding. Caley froze.

"St. Patrick and St. Mary!" he gasped.

The face vanished. Caley ran the entire tangled, slippery trail back to camp, praying all the while to St. Macartan, the patron of his family. In camp he immediately sought his Bible and fervently read that sacred book.

Francis returned to camp cold and bruised. He had spent most of the day slipping up and down Baker Mountain, but he was in high spirits.

"A demon I beheld," said Caley to his cousin.

"I think I found a promising bit of silver," said Francis. "Unfortunately it's on quite a steep slope. I'll have to wait till tomorrow before I can do much. This snow should be melted away by then."

"A demon I beheld," repeated Caley.

"Sure, lad. Where?"

"A wee bit up the creek I smelled sulfur. I leant over the water and there was the most horrible face," said Caley with a shiver.

"Only a reflection of your own, to be sure," returned Francis.

"Don't ye make light of it, cousin. 'Twas the ugliest specimen the divil might produce."

"Truly? Looked a bit like your mother, ay Caley?"

"Bite your biggity tongue, Francis! Don't ye dare malign me dearest mither. That's unlike ye. The lady may not 'ave been a looker but she warn't no divil either, I tell ye. Just go 'ave a look yourself an' tell me there ain't no divil there. The creek is strong of sulfur and the shore is bald of growth. A sure sign of the divil, it is."

In the morning Francis, Caley, and Henry went to the suspicious spot in the creek. The faint scent of sulfur mingled with the fragrance of the wet earth and shrubbery. Thin plumes of vapor disappeared into the air.

"By heaven, there it is!" said Francis. "I see the divil!"

Caley, in a low, monastic voice, indicated he saw it also. Henry Fry saw nothing in the clear water but the rocks and sand on the bottom. He told them the vapor and sulfur suggested nothing more than a thermal spring. The three of them returned to camp as the wind rose to a howl, driving snow before it.

Since the party was unequipped for snowy weather, they decided to winter over in Georgetown, several miles down Clear Creek.

Francis wanted to form a mining company consisting of himself, his cousin, the Killeen brothers, and Henry Fry. When spring came they would return to Kearney Gulch, for he believed the presence of the devil meant there was vast treasure to be had. Other prospectors had claimed spirits or angels led them to great mineral wealth, so why not devils? Francis appeared to relish the thought of fighting the devil for his silver.

The party spent the winter in a comfortable low cabin, discussing and refining their plans for a spring assault on the devil's sterling. Henry invited two other gentlemen to join the group, both of whom knew a good deal about how to tell silver ore from ordinary rocks and tree roots. Francis welcomed Herman Sprague and T.G. Woods as partners, choosing not to mention anything of the devil to them. Must not frighten the experts.

Spring arrived and the motley crew again journeyed up Kearney Gulch. They made camp in a small meadow just above the site where Kearney Creek passed sulfurous gas.

Early one morning Caley went down to the creek. He was stooping to examine the rocks on the bank when suddenly a hissing beast stood before him in the water. Its body was the size and shape of a man's, yet was distorted and twisted. The hair was like weeds tangled with black feathers, sticks, pebbles, and leaves. Sprouting from the body and black frock coat was gray moss, and the beast's bulging red eyes were locked on Caley, its lips drawn back in a snarl that showed long uneven fangs.

"St. Patrick and St. Mary!" whispered Caley, slowly rising to his feet. He fumbled in his pocket for his rosary and held the crucifix toward the approaching Thing at arm's length.

Knees shaking and hands quivering, Caley backed away, never removing his eyes from the beast. It hissed and salivated. Its hands drew up claw-like as it stiffly moved through the gurgling water toward the bank.

"O St. Patrick and St. Mary, save me!" choked Caley.

Steadily the demon approached. Not so steadily Caley retreated. He stumbled on rocks, grass, and branches, all the time holding up his cross. He fell backwards over a clump of weeds into the willow brush. Panic gripped him. Caley flew into the jumble of bushes that were growing in marshy soil. He lurched and crawled, fell and ran, getting wet and cold and breathless, until at last he made it to camp in near hysteria.

Caley was shaking violently. His face and arms were scratched and bleeding from the sharp branches. Tears were in his eyes. When he was finally calmed, Francis urged him to explain.

Caley told his fellow prospectors of the demon. He described it, saying he was sure it would have torn him apart.

Herman Sprague and T.G. Woods could only laugh and shake their heads. Henry Fry most certainly sighed. Shortly everyone returned to the business of locating a silver claim.

The following morning Timothy and Martin went down to the creek. They rejoined the others after several minutes in a shaken state similar to Caley's. They, too, had encountered the inhospitable vagrant in Kearney Creek. Only this time it had donned an opera cape, more appropriate attire in which to receive its distinguished guests. They described the creature as twice the size, twice as ugly, and twice as threatening. No longer claw-like, its hands were definite claws. No longer salivating, it now spit fire. The odor of sulfur in the air was nauseating, the water boiling, and the creek bottom littered with bones.

Herman Sprague and T.G. Woods nodded to one another. They had found no signs of silver in their several days of searching the area, and this demon business was an indication that the Irishmen were deranged; thus, they politely took their leave. Telling the Irishmen no silver was to be found there, they convinced only Henry Fry, who left with them.

Despite the lack of telegraph and telephone, news of the demon in Kearney Gulch reached many prospectors in Clear Creek Valley. From there the tale found its way to Central City's ears and Denver's saloons. Strangers would ask any Irishman they spotted if that Irishman saw the demon too. Would he be pleased to tell them about it?

Prospectors began to refer to that part of Kearney Gulch as the "Devil's Den." By now the air hung heavy with sulfurous gas and the sun never shone through the dense forest. The demon lay in wait in the water, its size increasing and shape altering each time it was mentioned. One pithy old prospector said he had gone up the creek and saw the thing, but it was no longer like a man. It was a huge dragon with scales and wings. The ground around it was putrid, covered with death and slime. Innocent, placid Kearney Creek was black and brackish. Another miner, M. Carroll, had also braved the forest to view the beast. It was absent when he arrived, but soon he heard it coming through the air. Two cows were writhing in its claws as it came toward Carroll. He raised a rifle and planted a bullet in the beast's breast. Maddened and dying, the dragon flew over the mountains, splashing into Grand Lake. Carroll, of course, heard the splash.

The demon story elicited a lot of laughter during its short life and several versions near the whiskey barrels, and Kearney Gulch seemed to suffer nothing from the brief inhabitation by the dragon. Needless to say, Francis Haverty and company found neither demon treasure nor honest silver in the gulch. Francis never found silver anywhere, except perhaps on the dinner table. He eventually gave up the adventurous life for the real estate business in Pueblo. His cousin, Caley, became disenchanted with America, and probably returned to his convent in County Waterford. The Killeen brothers later survived in Leadville as miners, a place they preferred to the peaceful sanitarium some folks suggested they might consider retiring to.

Kearney Gulch failed to yield silver for any other prospector. In later years its only inhabitants were a trapper who built a crude cabin in the upper section, marmots, deer, and a handful of men who operated a lumber mill about three quarters of a mile above the confluence of Kearney and Clear creeks.

Few signs remain of Kearney Creek's past visitors, and no signs of a sulfur spring. If there once was one, it has since dried up. There is a faint old road up to the lumber mill, where only gray piles of cut lumber and a few rusted parts of equipment mark the site. Farther up the gulch, the trapper's cabin rots into the grass. Farther still, Kearney Creek tumbles down from the lake in the bowl of Mt. Sniktau, where brilliant wildflowers carpet the treeless slopes and bright yellow warblers dart about for a few brief weeks in summer. Nowhere does the scent of sulfur mingle with the sweet fragrance of numerous flowers. Nowhere is Kearney Creek black and brackish.

The limpid, cold water reflects a crystal blue sky in its pools and sparkles like silver where it splashes in cataracts. It leaps into cool shadows, singing into sunlight, disappearing under boulders and fallen trees, to emerge again along soggy banks of lush moss and marsh marigolds, fresh, clear, melodious water...completely devil-free.

CHAPTER VI

A Determined Lover

"Will you be my own?" said J. Dawson Hidgepath in his tenderest, most refined Mississippi murmer. "Annie, Annie, you are my torment! Will you be my own?"

Annie sighed and slammed the door. She had no remorse in turning away the miner for the eleventh time. Ten times she had told him she would never, could never, be his wife. If he brought her roses in the dead of winter, she would turn him away. If he begged on his knees in the mud of Buckskin Joe's street, she would turn him away. It was her duty: Annie was Mrs. D.L. Lewis, and Mr. D.L. Lewis was usually no farther than the next room and never absent from Annie's heart.

Although Hidgepath was brokenhearted, his misery was brief. There were other women in the gold camp that was officially called Laurette and commonly referred to as Buckskin Joe or just plain Buckskin.

Gold was discovered in this narrow alpine valley eight miles northwest of Fairplay in August 1860 by Joseph Higginbottom, David Greist, M. Phillips, W.H.K. Smith, D. Berger, and A. Fairchild. The district and town were named for Higginbottom, a mountaineer and trapper known as "Buckskin Joe." For a few years the town was called Laurette, a combination of the names of the only ladies there in early 1861, Laura and Janette Dodge. They were the wives of the brothers Miles B. and Allen Dodge. As word of the gold discoveries spread, Laura and Janette were joined by other ladies, but the men in the area still outnumbered the ladies seventy-three to one.

When J. Dawson Hidgepath blew into Buckskin Joe in 1863 or 1864, he had to gaze on seventy-three bearded, bristly, gristly male faces before he saw the cherry lips and alabaster cheeks of one solitary damsel. Certainly gold enticed Hidgepath to the place with dreams of wealth and fame, yet deep within his soul he was nothing more than a great lover yearning for a lady all his own. Unfortunately, most of the ladies in Buckskin were married. Those who were unmarried were either twelve years old, crusty old grandmothers, or bawdy house girls. This rarely deterred Hidgepath.

Married, widowed, in the cradle or in the grave, as long as she was identifiable as female, J. Dawson Hidgepath was in love with her. And to this romantic Mississippian every woman in Buckskin was incredibly beautiful and beyond reproach.

Enamored, lovelorn Dawson wooed the ladies despite their remonstrations. He winked at them in the street. He sent them passionate letters. He gave them bouquets of flowers. He told them they were angelic and living images of Venus even if they had faces capable of freezing a plague of grasshoppers in mid-chomp. He arrived at their houses uninvited and unconcerned about their husbands or gentlemen friends.

Dawson's professed and intrusive love for Julia Cotton, a singer and dancer who performed in town, won him a violent dip in the creek at the hands of Miss Cotton's friends. Although Dawson could not mistake the intent of the dancer's bodyguards to inflict permanent injury, he resumed his passionate advances toward the lady until she left town. When he fell in love with Lulu Wise, which was probably at the same time he was in deep adoration of a half dozen other women, he annoyed the girl until she sought refuge in her employer. Miss Wise was a dance hall girl employed by scar-faced Hugh Melrose, who dealt with pests by stepping on them. Hidgepath was duly stepped on. To ease his crushed heart, Dawson made overtures to a lady staying at the Argyle House, until her broad and tall husband arrived in town, caressing a long-barreled revolver.

When Dawson was disengaged from the ladies and not occupied with evading their husbands, he worked as a miner in the Excelsior Mine and later the Argentum Mine. Undoubtedly, in every shovelful of dirt he saw a damsel's eyes. In every swing of the pick he heard a lady's voice.

On Sunday afternoon, 23 July 1865, Hidgepath went climbing up the toe of Mt. Bross, possibly in search of wildflowers for one of his angels. On the rocky, steep west side of the mountain he lost his footing and tumbled down several hundred feet, breaking his neck and other assorted bones. Later that day a prospector on Mt. Bross discovered Hidgepath's hat with its distinctive insignia (which may have been a family crest). A search party was organized, and J. Dawson Hidgepath's broken body was located in a rockslide area. His amorous career was over. His mortal remains were respectfully interred in the Buckskin Cemetery. Could a heart whose great love was unrequited rest peacefully in the grave? Perhaps Hidgepath's heart could, but his bones could not.

A short time after his burial Dawson's bones burrowed out of the narrow grave and made their way to a dance hall girl's room. The girl found the bones in her bed with Dawson's hat on top of them. Immediately the lovesick fellow was reburied.

Next J. Dawson Hidgepath called on Mrs. D.L. Lewis, although he was only the wreckage of his old self. One day there was a knock on the lady's door, and a letter forced beneath it. Mrs. Lewis read the love letter and opened the door in alarm. The clatter of a bleached, disconnected skeleton greeted her at her feet. The skull smiled from beneath Hidgepath's hat. "Will you be my own?" was whispered soft on the air. A loud scream issued from Mrs. Lewis's lungs as she sought relief in a faint. When she recovered she could only babble, "His bones...his ghost...his bones."

Month after month Hidgepath's bones poked through the grave grass and blazed a trail to ladies' doors, parlors, beds, and kitchens. Sometimes the visited lady heard an ardent profession of love whispered in the air. Sometimes the bones penned a passionate epistle. Sometimes they delivered a nosegay of wildflowers.

Month after month the men of Buckskin reburied the raffish bones. Once they dug a deeper grave, but to no avail. Next they put a large, flat rock on Dawson's tomb, but the bones sneaked out at the edge like a rodent caught in a springtime frenzy. Larger and heavier rocks were employed. The bones, lovelorn in every cell, continued to escape confinement to seek the gentler half of humanity.

When the town of Buckskin Joe faded into obscurity and the wives and mothers went to sunnier places with their husbands and sons, J. Dawson Hidgepath sought the fair ladies of Alma, a boomtown less than two miles east of Buckskin, which sprang up in 1872-73. The saloonkeepers' wives, dance hall girls, traders' wives, an old laundress, the laundress's granddaughter, and a mercantile storekeeper's wife were included in the amorous advances of Hidgepath's bones. Again his words of love hovered in the air. Again he appeared skeletally clad, nestled in pillows as if he wished dearly to be similarly nestled on warm bosoms.

One of the ladies, who was afflicted with poor eyesight, found the notorious bones in her kitchen. She mistook them for soup bones, and into the simmering broth pot they were tossed. Fortunately her husband discovered the gentleman's femur in his dinner bowl in time to have Hidgepath properly reburied.

When the saloonkeeper found his wife peacefully sleeping beside the deceased Hidgepath's yellowed scaffolding, the man tossed the bones out to his dog. The dog buried them for future snacking, but the bones dug themselves out and scampered off to another lady's dwelling.

Telling tales of J. Dawson Hidgepath's bones grew to be an art among the miners and frosty old mountain men. In the way of clever advances, the bones outshone anything Lothario accomplished. Sometimes when Dawson spied two or more ladies to be courted, he wasted no precious moments by calling on one at a time. Taking a bouquet, the radius and ulna sauntered off to one lady, while a letter-bearing tibia and fibula went to see another. And since there were few ladies in Alma, Hidgepath's bones tramped down to Fairplay a time or two. Whenever the adoring bones were discovered, they were quickly returned to the grave in Buckskin Cemetery and new means to keep them there were adopted.

Finally in 1880 townsmen decided enough was enough. Under cover of night a handful of citizens removed J. Dawson Hidgepath's wandering skeleton, took a midnight mule ride over Mosquito Pass, and on the outskirts of Leadville pitched the bones into an outhouse. That would certainly take care of the skeletal Don Juan, they reasoned. If he could possibly climb out of the hole, he would be too ashamed to call on the ladies, for no gentleman desired to be identified with the fragrance of Backhouse No. V.

No longer were the wives and mothers and dance hall girls of Alma and Fairplay inconvenienced by their boney lover. No longer did Hidgepath pen love letters or pluck flowers for them. It appeared the lovesick miner's malady had been remedied at last.

One day a Leadville lady visited the privy where J. Dawson Hidgepath languished in oblivion. No sooner had she entered when from the aromatic depths she heard a tender Mississippi murmur, "Will you be my own?"

CHAPTER VII

From Mozart To Mules

 utwardly unimpressive in its gray monotony, Brown Gulch, a quarter of a mile west of Silver Plume, has long been cluttered with an ethereal population. Through some abnormality of the rocks or the artifice of an unhinged hummingbird, nearly everything and everyone who has died there has remained to haunt the place. From the English gentleman at the top who loves to perform Mozart's violin sonatas on windy nights, to the incorrigible pair of mules at the bottom who love to bray on those same windy nights, Brown Gulch has never lacked entertainment.

The first human to take advantage of immortality in the gulch was a moldy old prospector named Jack (John or Amos) Strong, known to those who avoided him as Mad Jack. Mad Jack was a disillusioned Fortyniner who came to Colorado in 1859 or thereabout hoping to get his muddy fingers into some gold dust. But Jack seemed to be one of the most unlucky men in the territory. He found nothing in Cherry Creek, nothing in the Gregory diggings, nothing at Tarryall or California Gulch. When the silver discoveries of upper Clear Creek heralded a new era in 1865, old Mad Jack was itching for wealth and probably for a good bath—hadn't had one in years, except when he was caught in a rainstorm back in '58.

In autumn of 1865 Jack was grubstaked by some Irishmen, whom he quickly found an excuse to desert, and went in search of his silver buttons. With his favorite old "bur-ruh," as moldy and as aromatic as Jack and allegedly fathered by a moose, Mad Jack poked into the vertical, yet-unnamed gulch where his burro led him. He trusted whole-heartedly in the metallurgical expertise of the beast and made camp.

Although Mad Jack was hard put to set eyes on any silver seam, he refused to give up. After all, his burro had indicated silver was to be found there. When he ran out of flour because he was stuffing too many buckwheat cakes into his pack animal, he lived several weeks on beans and sap and possibly on hummingbird stew when that was available. Finally, the old fellow found some promising blossom rock and was so excited after all those dry years that, in his haste to begin mining, he blew himself and his burro into the next kingdom with a faulty charge.

A short time later, J.M. Eckhart, William Brown, Samuel Watson, and their cohorts arrived in the gulch. What little was left of Mad Jack and his burro was properly interred to insure that scavenging hummingbirds wouldn't use them for nest material. But Jack found it impossible to rest in peace with the hordes of prospectors tramping over his claim. His spirit rose up to stake the silver seam with phantom signs. By day other prospectors heard the uncanny chink-chink-chink of Jack's pick at the site and sometimes heard the complaining of an unseen burro. By night the white, luminous form of Mad Jack hovered ominously by his claim, with his white, luminous burro faithfully hovering at his side. The prospector's ghost would chase off any trespassers with a long stick. Brown Gulch, now named, was turned inside out and upside down with silver mines stuffed in every niche, but the ghosts of Mad Jack and his burro remained to hamper operations.

Brown Gulch acquired its second ghost on 23 October 1877, when a greedy miner assassinated Stephen Pierce at the Mammoth Mine. Afterwards, every red-blooded miner at the Mammoth saw Pierce's ghost rise up in the moonlight to stand at the mine entrance, watching over them. As considerate in rigor mortis as he was in life, Pierce protected the miners from many disasters, including a fire one spring night in the bunk house.

Soon after, a pair of mules was added to the ghostly population of Brown Gulch. In May of 1879, Peter Reedy was leading a string of mules laden with cable up to the Montreal Mine when the trail dirt, saturated with spring rain, gave way. The two front mules tumbled several hundred feet to the bottom of the gulch and were killed instantly. When twilight fell that day, Reedy and his friend, William Goking, heard the sound of braying jackasses where the pair had hit bottom. The men investigated, finding no mules in sight. From then on, when Reedy passed the spot he heard the braying of his deceased mules. Other miners, especially Cornishmen who had been too long at the Fox and Hound Saloon, claimed to hear the braying mules. A few besotted chaps stood singing at the spot one hot night, and the voices of the ghost jackasses chimed in, taking the baritone.

Another singing ghost in Brown Gulch was A.E. McBride's dog. In life the Kerry Blue Terrier couldn't resist singing when his master sang. The two often entertained the miners at the Fox and Hound and were invited to sing at Mary Lampshire's piano in the Lampshire

hotel. One day the Kerry consumed a morsel unfit for canine diges-
tion (probably a hummingbird) and quickly met his end. McBride,
whose temper was phenomenal, told the Kerry he had no right to "up
and die." He ordered the dog to come back, and, according to
McBride, the Kerry promptly obeyed. Unfortunately, he could no
longer sing. He only hummed.

A year after the Kerry's demise, Brown Gulch produced two more
ghosts in one month. On 4 July 1885, Louis Chio was shot dead in
Brownville, and his ghost was seen one day by girls returning home
from school. Then on 31 July, a confused, unhappy man who had
been a Confederate soldier in the Civil War took his own life. The
man was William Neff, an Arkansas native who thought to begin
anew in the Colorado Rockies, taking employment at the Telephone
Mine on Brown Mountain. He was a quiet, industrious man, but on
the day of his death he told his employer, Mr. Saltzman, that he
didn't feel like working anymore that morning. He went to the cabin
near the mine and blew his head off with a stick of dynamite, having
first covered his head with a quilt. Saltzman found the mangled corpse
at noon and was aghast at the horrible sight of blood spattered over
the cabin walls. Neff was respectfully interred in the cemetery, but for
many months miners passing the cabin said they heard terrible ut-
terances and desperate weeping, as if Neff's spirit were within. The
cabin came to be regarded as an unholy, haunted place, avoided by
most of the men.

Despite those darkest of moments when men and women destroyed
themselves, the boom days of Brown Gulch were full of song and
cheer. The Cornish miners sang on their way to and from work. The
Italian miners sang all day Sunday and on the feast day of St. Lucy.
Everyone sang on Saturday night at the bar or at the Lampshire
hotel. Lizzie Griffin and her naked cousins taught the men a new
song or two about bedbugs and sent them home whistling like tea-
pots. Who needed an opera house when the entire gulch could perform *The Barber of Seville?* There was song from every corner, even
from James Cheyne's Granite Polishing Works, and in the decade of
the 1880s Brownville discovered a favorite, although they never told
him so. He was no singer, but he was a fine violinist who could move
the Cornishmen to tears when he rendered Mendelssohn's Concerto
in E Minor or the music of Mozart's symphonies. The favorite was
Clifford Griffin (no relation to Lizzie), who was a wan, thin, yet
handsome gentleman from England.

When Clifford met an untimely death 19 June 1887 and was buried on a cliff near the Seven Thirty Mine at 10,451 feet, tales began to fly. In no time, an ordinary Englishman with a violin had become a legend. Countless tales about his life, habits, past, and death, about his brother, the Seven Thirty Mine, and mysterious dead brides sailed through the air. Yarn spinners made him everything from a groveling sot to a melancholy baronet, having him murdered by his brother, murdered by the Seven Thirty's foreman or bookkeeper, or dispatched at his own hand. Even the suicide tales came in many inspired shapes and colors. A popular one claimed Clifford blasted himself a cozy grave in the granite outcropping overlooking Brown Creek. When the grave was ready, the Englishman played a wildly sad tune on his violin, shot himself, and fell into the hole. Miners, hearing the shot, rushed to the scene and buried Clifford where he lay.

Later, a nine-foot, seven-inch granite monument was placed on the cliff above Brownville for all to see, reminding the citizens that their favorite violinist was gone. But of course in Brown Gulch nobody remained dead for long. Clifford commenced his ethereal violin music before the first anniversary of his death. He played from the lofty place where he was interred, filling the night air with mysterious melodies. Anyone with an ounce of superstition in him heard the music, and anyone possessing more than an ounce saw the ghost himself. Although the ghosts of the sonorous mules were close seconds, Clifford's ghost became the most popular specter in Brown Gulch, and remains so to this day.

Local legend said windy nights were especially favorable to his violin concerts. Yet Clifford didn't limit himself to any particular time. He played on quiet nights in December or balmy afternoons in July. Sometimes he was seen on the edge of his cliff, a dignified gentleman in a hazy light, serenely drawing the bow across the strings of his violin. He made his presence especially known on the anniversary of his death, loitering around the monument in his best black wool coat, blue silk waistcoat, and impeccable derby, casually enjoying a cigar. Curiously, a fresh bouquet of flowers also appeared on 19 June, placed at the foot of the granite memorial. In the beginning, the flowers were sent by Griffin's brother, yet they arrived each anniversary long after the brother died. The music, the mystery, the wonder, and the secret of Clifford Griffin, buried high above Silver Plume, has brought many a resident and tourist the mile-and-a-half hike to his grave to experience that once-in-a-lifetime moment when his ghost transcends the bonds of time.

Although Griffin was the favorite ghost in Brown Gulch, he was not the last. The spirit population increased by three, 22 February 1899. At four in the morning, an avalanche thundered down Brown Mountain, ripping through the Seven Thirty's ore house where Ben Nelson, John Anderson, and Peter Olsen were sleeping in a second-floor room. The snowslide also hit Dan Fitzpatrick's cabin nearby. Screaming and flailing, the men were dragged by the mass of snow down Brown Gulch with the machinery, rock, and wreckage, and buried out of sight. Olsen was the only man dug out alive. Fitzpatrick's body was located the next day. In the spring, Nelson's body was discovered by B.C. Catren, Sr. when he noticed a human foot protruding from a bank of thawing snow in the gulch. The unfortunate Mr. Anderson was never recovered.

On 22 February the year following, the spirits of the three deceased miners turned up at the Seven Thirty workings. They moaned around the windows of the buildings, rattled doors, disturbed the sleep of the few men living there, and behaved in traditional ghostly fashion. It was not recorded if they continued this as an annual practice.

Prior to the turn of the century, Brownville, whose population had dwindled from that of a thriving boomtown to less than 100 residents, was knocked on her ear by the Seven Thirty's massive tailings. In 1892 and 1895 the dump was loosened by excess water from the spring thaw, but caused no fatalities. The earlier slide knocked down several mine buildings, blocked a few tunnel entrances, and buried William Payne's house and two railroad cars of quarried granite on the track at the Terrible Mill. The latter slide destroyed the old Lampshire boarding house and demolished Mrs. Desmoineaux's house and the Terrible Mill, leaving the rest of Brownville in peace. But the Seven Thirty's dump finished the job in 1912, burying forever the unpretentious gulch town.

From 1895 to 1912 the worthless rock from the Seven Thirty's sixteen miles of tunnels had again built up an immense dump in the upper crotch of Brown Gulch, stretching for 800 feet in some sections. Several times the dump slung rocks at Brownville, carrying out the finale on 24 June 1912, when rain and thawing snow saturated the entire mass, loosening it slowly overnight. By morning thousands of tons of rock, mud, and logs had gouged down the gulch.

Oscar Johnson, who was living in the cabin at the Seven Thirty, barely escaped ghosthood, saving only his watch and a few clothes before his cabin was wrenched into the gulch. The ore house, blacksmith shop, and machinery at the mine were also destroyed by the slide.

Taking out cabins and the buildings of the Dunderberg and other mines along the way, the moving mass of rock and mud sloshed down the gulch slowly enough to allow men, women, children, and dogs to escape. As the deluge folded over the Lampshire hotel, witnesses claimed to have heard the piano plinking, giving rise to rumors that someone was buried alive, a sort of Nero who fiddled while Brownville burned. In the end only two men, John Custer and John Williams, were missing, their shared cabin demolished, but it was believed they had left the area before the slide hit. If they had not, they undoubtedly would appear as specters. In any case, no one would be digging for them. No one dug for anything. The gray mound that once was Brownville was left behind. The only residents who remained were of the foggy class, those phantom mules and phantom men, and possibly a phantom piano. A highway engineer, Merritt B. Smith, said he heard the piano playing during a road improvement project in 1957.

There is little left to remind passersby that Brownville once clung to the gulch, except scattered fragments of rusted machinery, a rotted shoe, china shards, and the vestiges of a stone wall fading into the gray of the tailings. Stubborn raspberry bushes and the emerald flash of hummingbirds are all that brighten the desolate and steep ravine. The air is dry, the dust is gray, Brown Creek babbles and gibbers like an insipid old washerwoman, and those rambunctious, courageous, excessive, singing characters who gave life to the place are gone. Sadly gone.

And yet, something in the wind sounds like Cornish miners singing around the piano...and mules braying...and the cussing of Mad Jack...and the strains of a violin. Can it be only the wind? Have Brownville's citizens come back? Certainly no; Brownville's citizens never left.

CHAPTER VIII

The Cheater

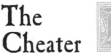 hen the Union Pacific Railroad advanced to Julesburg (a station later called Weir, a short distance from the present Julesburg) in June 1867, behind it galloped, slithered, and trundled hundreds of assorted adventurers and entrepreneurs. During the next few months, while the railroad clawed its way to Cheyenne, Wyoming, Julesburg swelled with indefatigable activity.

Immigrants to the gold fields, freighters, railroad workers, capitalists, outlaws, thugs, and assassins gathered and dispersed at the spot as if winds blew them in and winds blew them out again. They came from the East and disappeared anonymously into the vastness of the West. Consisting mostly of men, Julesburg's volatile population awarded her temporary life as a town of shanties, covered wagons, tents, and sometimes as many as several thousand people. Besides honest merchantmen, there were many more-or-less permanent residents of the town who engaged in the necessary trades of gambling, pocket-picking, brawling, and murdering. In this class of businessmen was a Mr. Brown, an independent profiteer whose house of trade, a large canvas tent, suspiciously appeared to have been borrowed from the U.S. Cavalry. Brown's favorite hat was burdened with the same suspicion.

Brown stocked his tent with the basic necessities, which he sold at a painful price and much sacrifice to himself. He conducted transactions with his hands preoccupied by the gleaming U.S. Army sidearms hanging on his hips and his mouth working at a plug or two of tobacco. Though exhibiting an allergic reaction to lawmen (which were scarce) and hemp (which was never far off), Brown was otherwise an ordinary Julesburg citizen. When the profits of his "general store" were slow in turning, he converted his tent into a gambling den, which was an eminently satisfactory undertaking begun each afternoon and lasting half the night.

An associate of Brown's was John Hatch, usually referred to as Professor Hatch, among other things, or The Professor, a title having little to do with academics. The Professor, who hailed from Philadelphia, sold a patent medicine to weary and ill travelers. This vital elixir could cure anything from impotency to rheumatism, whichever the potential customer appeared to be suffering from, and even protect a man from sudden death. Rumor had it that the Professor sold several bottles to an immigrant family enroute to Denver, promising them that the medicine, if taken in large doses, would repel Indians.

One hot afternoon in August, Brown and Hatch were conducting a poker game in the cavalry tent. A large man named Valery, who had more whiskers than head, was attempting to win back several of his mules and one of two supply wagons from Brown. He was proceeding miserably. Three other gentlemen in the game, Olney Nangle, Harry Endriken, and William MacLean, were holding their own, while a fat man with struggling pores and a naked face, calling himself "Gabby," looked on.

There was much smoking, drinking, and growling as the game wore toward evening. At one point, Valery banged down his cards with a celebrating oath, for the winning hand had returned to him four of his mules. He was persuaded to go for the rest while a great black thunderhead grumbled on the northwestern horizon.

By nightfall Valery was losing mules again, and the thunderstorm was assaulting Julesburg with torrential rain and wind. Gabby had fallen into a sleep induced by the Professor's elixir, and the Professor appeared to be considering the same exercise as he swilled the medicine and nodded and winked in the lantern light. MacLean exhibited signs of having a bottomless bank account as he merrily played and merrily lost, while Endriken decided to simply watch for a spell.

The men were about to begin another game when a stranger entered the tent with a wet gust of wind following him. He removed his soaking topcoat and tossed it on the snoring Gabby.

"Room for another?" he said.

"Got money?" said Brown, shutting up one eye to survey the stranger.

The man grinned. He slid his hand into his breast pocket and withdrew a bundle of banknotes. He replaced the money, still grinning.

Brown nodded, indicating a crate opposite.

"What do they call you" said Brown.

"Pierce," was the indifferent reply.

Soon the game was under way, and Pierce, with his dripping hat pulled down low on his brow, grinned at Brown till that businessman felt fairly annoyed at the display of teeth. He played with the ease of a man confident of winning every game.

Pierce did win the first hand. He also won the second. When he won the third, Brown brought his hand down on the table with an ugly curse. MacLean and Nangle laughed aloud, happy to see Brown could be beaten, even if he was beaten by someone other than themselves. Gabby awoke with the noise and spent many a jealous moment staring at Pierce's mustache.

A crash of thunder uncomfortably near only served to intensify Brown's determination to prevail against the stranger. The stakes were raised. Professor Hatch took more interest in the game. Gabby drew his chair nearer for better observation.

Lightning flashed. Thunder roared. The tent roof sagged where rain puddles collected. Brown spat more frequently, and Nangle chuckled to himself and sat up a bit straighter.

As the night grew soggier, Pierce continued to win. He grinned broadly at Brown, saying, "I've played more challenging games with toddlers."

"Toddlers," repeated Brown, making that innocent word an oath.

From that point, Nangle and Endriken watched every breath, every twitch of Pierce. If he were cheating, they were certain to spot it. Yet despite their hawk's eyes, the stranger once again placed a winning hand of aces and kings on the table.

"Cheater!" proclaimed John Hatch, making a move toward violence.

"Professor!" interposed Nangle as Endriken placed a restraining hand on John Hatch's shoulder. "Don't do anything, it's an honest hand. I watched him every minute. No way could he cheat, confound him."

"No way," confirmed Gabby.

"Not unless he's a magician," added Harry Endriken.

Professor Hatch allowed himself a vicious glare at Pierce and sat down. Squinting at the stranger, Brown ground his teeth and spat a stream of juice after the word "toddlers" escaped him. The game continued.

The next hand, Valery passed and MacLean called. Pierce again displayed a winning full house with three aces.

"Damn cheater!" cried the Professor, and he flew at Pierce.

A scuffle ensued in which Valery knocked down John Hatch and Gabby knocked himself down. Pierce was untouched, grinning.

"I'll prove you're cheating," said the Professor. "Luck doesn't deal a man aces every hand."

He searched quickly through the remaining cards and drew out several aces that matched Pierce's. Professor Hatch threw the cards in the stranger's face.

All in one moment the Professor struck at Pierce while Valery pushed him away and Pierce's hand made a slight move toward his coat. In that instant, Brown had drawn his revolver, shooting the stranger. Pierce took the bullet in his breast.

Grabbing his chest, Pierce staggered forward. His eyes met Brown's and he grinned. He reached across the table toward his assassin, his hand wet with blood. Deep red drops fell on Pierce's winning cards as the man doubled over, but before he hit the ground he had vanished from their sight.

There was a grave silence in the tent save for the patter of the rain that had dwindled to a gentle shower. The men stood about as if each had just been supplied with a noose to try on for size, alterations free of charge. No one looked at another. No one wanted to be first to put words to the event. They stared at the ground, at the bloodstained cards, at the spot where Pierce's body should have been.

Pierce was gone. Pierce's topcoat was gone. The men could only stare.

A gust of summer wind flipped open the tent door. The lantern on the ceiling pole began to swing. The cards on the table were lifted up and slung into Brown's face as a sound like laughter started there and went out at the door. Brown, in a livid rage, rushed out after it, cursing, screaming, and was seen no more in Julesburg.

More than thirty years later in December 1899, Pierce, or a stranger very much like him, entered a gambling establishment in Denver to play poker and faro. This man won too many hands for the comfort of the other gamblers and soon was declared a cheater. A brawl followed. The man was shot. With a remarkable grin, the stranger disappeared into the smoky air.

All that remained of him was a full house with three bloodstained aces.

CHAPTER IX

"Thou shalt not covet thy neighbor's wife."

For a Fistful of Oysters

 or thy neighbor's oysters. Both wives and oysters were a rare sight in the early mining days of Colorado, and some men not only covetted them, they were willing to kill for them. Indeed, a man would put a bullet through another for a can of slimy oysters.

It was a strong hankering for the bivalve mollusks that got the better of Edward Bainbridge, induced him to shoot a man in Georgetown in 1867, and led to Bainbridge's eventual career as a ghost.

Edward Bainbridge, an ill-mannered Scotsman with an ungovernable temper when he was drunk, had set out to find his gold mine in the West. He arrived in St. Louis safely, but having a weakness for errant women and poker games, he lost most of his traveling money. He also indulged in the luxury of fresh Atlantic oysters for the last time.

Undaunted by his losses and the uncertainty of what lurked beyond St. Louis, Bainbridge gathered himself up and managed to make it to Denver. In the "Queen City" he boasted of how he had bargained and swindled his way across the endless prairies. Unfortunately, there was no gold scattered about the city, and he found himself penniless in the streets. They were dusty streets, sometimes muddy. And for Bainbridge, they were lonely streets. He found himself a prostitute. Persuading her to work on a pay-later plan, he secured from her some grub, whiskey, and a warm bed for the night. By dawn she had discovered the Scotsman had no money and propelled him into the street in his longjohns, slinging his clothes after him. The door slammed. Bainbridge hurried into his clothes, but no sooner had he pulled on his boots than the woman again flung herself upon him, knocking him down. A small, amused audience watched as she screamed and pulled Bainbridge's red beard. She had to make a living too, and he had better quite well get out of town because she had friends. Big friends. He escaped down the street feeling like a plucked rooster.

A short time later Edward Bainbridge won a man's horse and gold pocket watch at a card game. He crowed at his change of luck and disturbed passersby with his abrasive laughter. He set out to find his gold mine.

The next time he stained the chronicles of Colorado, he was attempting to swindle four brothers out of their placer claim near Spanish Bar. A man who practiced claim jumping was a ripe candidate for a hemp noose. The four brothers opted for pounding the Scot's head. He was only fool enough to face four raging buffalo at once when he was under the influence of Taos Lightning, and being sober at the decisive moment, knew he was better off elsewhere. He made an appearance in Black Hawk and a few other camps in the region.

Having altogether lost the taste for claim jumping, Bainbridge actually worked some of the scraggy gulches, but he never hit paydirt. He remained genial when not drinking but otherwise engaged in brawls, threats, loud boasting, and louder laughing. One could easily find him at brothels or poker games, usually not doing very well at either. He blamed his elusive luck on excessive hard work and hard whiskey. He began to spend less time with a shovel in his hands and more time with cards in his hands. He was sinking into a vulgar, reckless life, and he thoroughly enjoyed it.

News of rich silver discoveries in the upper Clear Creek area enticed Bainbridge out of the bawdy houses to look for a silver seam of his own. It was the spring of 1865. He was starting over again in another rough camp, another rush for wealth.

In the camp called Georgetown, Edward Bainbridge thought the beavers possessed more silver than did the frenzied men poking holes in the mountains. The beavers "had to git." Some wound up in stew as more prospectors poured into the valley, more silver was discovered, and more timber was chopped down. The town exploded with activity. Where the beavers had been a city was platted.

With several partners, Bainbridge worked a silver vein that summer and the following year on Griffith Mountain. It was enough to support them, but not enough to make any of them a silver king. Bainbridge easily slipped back into his old habits (not that he had actually abandoned them). His loud manner made him well known in the city, yet he was not totally disliked. His moments of charm and Scotch humor gained him friends. The English aristocrats and Southern gentlemen in Georgetown tolerated his bizarre behavior and brashness, amused by his wild antics when he was drunk...as long as he threatened or injured no one.

The Scotsman's silver seam eventually dwindled to mud. His partners migrated to another territory. He became a desperate fellow, drinking more and threatening to dislodge certain portions of the anatomy of any person who got in his way. But most Georgetown citizens, full of enthusiasm for their new city and too busy for idle nonsense, brushed off the bothersome Scot as if he were a mosquito.

By the spring of 1867, Edward Bainbridge had made a complete nuisance of himself. Several times a week he was tossed out of saloons for vicious behavior. On Tuesday, 23 April 1867, he drew his revolver on Mr. Osborn of Georgetown, threatening to blow his head off. A couple of other men interfered in time to save Mr. Osborn. That afternoon Bainbridge met an acquaintance, James Martin, and flew at him, threatening to shoot him. Martin was accustomed to the Scotsman's explosive displays and, laughing it off, was found the next day playing cards with him. Martin was an inoffensive, mild-mannered gentleman. He usually humored Bainbridge, taking the noise and threats as jokes. After all, did the Scot ever carry them through?

On Wednesday afternoon the two men were playing a quiet game of seven-up in John Mickle's saloon on the corner of Fourth and Rose streets. Bainbridge had offered to give Martin three points in the game if he would play him for a can of oysters. Oysters were a coveted item, and the nearest thing to them in landlocked Colorado Territory was the unpalatable freshwater clam that sucked mud in the prairie lakes. Pitiful clams. When oysters were available they were canned or sauced and outrageously priced. Fresh mollusks would not arrive on the scene for another year or so, when they could be shipped via the railroad to Cheyenne, packed in barrels of salt water with ice and cornmeal to keep them fresh and plump.

Oysters were uppermost in Bainbridge's thoughts while the game of seven-up progressed. It began as a friendly game. The two men drank and laughed. Then, when Martin won the first hand, Bainbridge's mood changed. The Scotsman exclaimed with an oath that he would shoot Martin should Martin win the second. Martin had heard all that before and went on to win the second game, his last card scarcely hitting the table before Edward Bainbridge drew his revolver, pointed it directly in the astonished gentleman's face, and pulled the trigger.

James Martin was sprawled on the floor, his face burned by the powder and bleeding profusely. The bullet had gone through his nose and lodged in his brain. He was immediately put into the care of Dr. Aduddel, and Bainbridge was as quickly arrested.

The Scot was locked in a second-floor room of a house...without the can of oysters. The arresting officers guarded the floor below.

When it became apparent to the Georgetown citizenry that James Martin would not live, they became incensed at the thought of a brutal murderer in their midst. A large crowd of men secured the nearest rope—a clothes line—and gathered at the house where Bainbridge was held about ten o'clock that night. A few entered the upper window and seized Bainbridge. He was hurled out of the window to the ground, where he was bound by the waiting vigilance committee.

Bainbridge protested loudly at his mistreatment. He believed he deserved a trial. The vigilantes assured him this *was* his trial.

"You can't hang me!" yelled the raging Bainbridge. "Should you dare, I'll haunt you the rest of your bloody lives! By thunder you can't hang me!"

Bainbridge tried to escape. He fought. He kicked. He cursed. He yelled at the top of his voice as the crowd fastened the rope around his neck and dragged him to a nearby pine.

"By God you can't hang me!" he yelled, more full of anger than fear. "I'll haunt you! I swear I'll haunt all of you and all your kin after you! You can't hang me!"

They could and they did. Without further ado the Scotsman was hoisted up, and, kicking and fighting mad to the end, he strangled to death. His neck was unbroken.

"Leave 'im to the devil," they said.

The following morning Edward Bainbridge was cut down, and his remains were buried not far from the spot, just below the Point of Rocks. According to tradition, he was the first to grace the cemetery. But his interment was brief. Someone dug him up and sold the corpse to a Central City doctor, who kept the skeleton on display for a long time in his office.

Meanwhile, James Martin surprised his fellow citizens and recovered. Although he had a disfigured face and was plagued by headaches, he lived a normal life in the district for many years. It was not recorded if he claimed his can of oysters. One thing was for certain: Edward Bainbridge would never touch another oyster. Or would he?

The year after his demise, Edward returned. He was only a shade of his former self, true to his final vow. His first appearance was in August 1868, when he went rampaging through the house where he had earlier been incarcerated. He unlocked doors, blew out lanterns, and banged cupboards in the kitchen. The shocked occupants thought it was a violent disturbance of the wind until they heard the laughter. The deceased Scot's distinctive laugh echoed through the kitchen defiantly, and it went out of the house to the fatal pine hard by.

A gentleman living in the house told Georgetowners of the strange occurence. They shrugged it off, telling him of a peaceful sanitarium in Connecticut.

"Sanitariums be blowed! There's a ghost in that house!"

As the nightly entertainment continued through autumn, more of the town's citizens were convinced something was happening there. Many scoffed at the presence of Bainbridge's ghost or any ghost whatsoever, yet they had no explanation for the evidence before them. Lanterns went out or shattered. Bolted doors flew open. Contents of cupboards were suddenly slung onto the floor. One of the occupants, a man respected in the community, was thrown out of his bed in the middle of the night. No one laughed at him when he told of his experience. The bizarre events so disconcerted the residents that they were forced to abandon the house. Other persons keeping night vigils at the place witnessed the same activity. They too were unable to explain the mystery.

One night a women among them screamed, "There he is!" as they all saw a figure of a man slip around a corner into another room.

One of the gentlemen present, Ernest Campbell, dashed after the figure, believing it was another of the party playing tricks. He pursued the form through the parlor, out the door, and toward the pine on which Bainbridge had been hanged. When Campbell was nearly upon him, the figure turned, a grin on its vaporous countenance, a rope knotted around its neck. Then it was gone.

Campbell returned to his companions, pale and shaken. He told them of his encounter with Bainbridge; he had seen him in life and had no doubt the ghostly figure was the Scotsman. To avoid having his constitution tried so severely again, Campbell swore never to return to the house.

On 24 December 1868, the local newspaper, the *Miner*, printed the full tale, identifying the ghost as Edward Bainbridge, saying he was "doomed for a certain term to walk the night, and for the day confined to fast in fire, till the foul crimes done in his days of 'nature' are burnt and purged away." Proud of the city's ghost, the *Miner* concluded: "Georgetown is now ahead of any town in the Territory in the ghost and haunted house line. Denver and Central must look to their laurels." Denver and Central had a multitude of ghosts of which the *Miner's* editor must have been unaware; nevertheless, his ghost story encouraged the spectators to wait at the house for the translucent Mr. Bainbridge. Likewise, the *Rocky Mountain News*, snatching up the story, enticed visitors to the spot.

Numerous persons witnessed the door-banging and other phenomena at the house for the next several months. Some were terrified. Some were amused. Some insisted the activity was a result of the wind...even when the wind was absent. Most of the time the disturbances were confined to the house, but on occasion the energy present loitered about the towering pine, shaking the tree in a frenzy. Believers were certain the ghost caused the tree to shake. Nonbelievers were just as certain blasting in the mines was the reason it shook. No one could prove either theory.

Although the frequency of his visits had declined in 1869, Edward Bainbridge continued to make his presence known. On dares schoolboys would wait for the ghost at dusk in the untenanted house. Often the boys fled in terror after only a few minutes in the shadowy rooms. Then by 1871, with only two previous disturbances in 1870, the door-banging ceased altogether. Edward Bainbridge gradually faded from memory, and eventually the frame house was torn down.

On 24 April 1887, exactly twenty years since the day Bainbridge was hanged, a girl was near the Point of Rocks looking for her kitten. She saw a bearded gentleman sitting on the ground. Gracie Mills, fourteen, approached the man, intending to ask him if he had seen her pet. As she went a few yards nearer, she realized she could distinguish rocks and weeds right through him, and she noticed a knotted rope around his neck. Gracie shuddered.

The apparition spoke to the child, making a simple request. In a fright, Gracie turned on her heel and ran home. She told her parents of the strange man, describing the rope, his beard, and his voice. She said earnestly she was not making up any of the story.

Because Gracie never heard of Edward Bainbridge, her parents, though reluctant to believe in ghosts, believed the child was telling the truth. They believed her especially when Gracie explained what the phantom had requested of her.

He had asked for a can of oysters.

CHAPTER X

The Spectral Associates of Mining Men

or sheer quantity of ghosts, gases, and goblins, the mining profession undoubtedly fetched the prize. The mine without a ghost was a mine without miners, and most shafts were not content with one ghost; they required several. The population of supernatural creatures was so thick in some mines that it was no curiosity if the miners got them caught in their nostrils when taking in a breath.

There is evidence that every miner packed his own particular favorites in his Gladstone bag and dragged them from boomtown to boomtown, setting up housekeeping for them in the damp mines and noisy mills. In 1889, a ghastly ghost with a blown-off arm was seen wandering through the Stevens Mine on McClellan Mountain, Clear Creek County. A few years later, when the miner who first saw it emigrated, this precise ghost was discovered in Leadville's Chippewa No. Six Mine. A similar apparition appeared in the Mamie R. Mine on Raven Hill in Cripple Creek.

The Mamie R. had a bad reputation in 1894, in part due to two fatalities the previous summer. Tommyknockers were rife in this mine, as they were in every mine, but this particular breed of those mischievous sprites possessed villainous dispositions. Instead of saving miners from danger, as was their calling, the Mamie R. Tommyknockers invited men toward it. With a relish. They jumped up and down on beams with a determined pounding until the beams collapsed. They snapped cables. They caused premature blasts. And the horrible one-armed ghost was probably a cohort of these little wretches or something of their devising.

When the ghost was first seen, it appeared to be a miner. He walked into charged shot and, after the dust settled, came forth covered with gore, holding his blown-off arm over his shoulder. The miners grabbed at him, catching space. In shock they watched him calmly walk to the bucket hoist, pull the bell cord, and go up. The engineer working the hoist never saw him and was unable to answer the questioning miners as to his departing direction, while those vulgar Tommyknockers snickered from the crossbeams.

A ghost common to many mines was that of the miner who had met death in a particular mine. The spirit of such a hapless man exhibited neurotic tendencies to repeat his tragic end ceaselessly—getting blown up or crushed once was hardly sufficient. Perhaps this was as a warning to the living, or perhaps all his energy was caught in that last moment and had yet to dissipate. A miner killed in the Morning Star Mine near Leadville returned for many years in the struggle and precise location of his agonizing death until that portion of the shaft was sealed up. He may indulge in that exercise yet.

A less repetitious pair of miners, Sebastian Zang and William Vine, appeared after their deaths to save other miners from disaster. These two men drowned in the Bates Mine at Black Hawk on 7 August 1885 after an explosion filled the shaft they were in with water. While in spirit form they saved one miner from an explosion, another from a fall, and several at once from a cave-in, where the survivors claimed they witnessed Zang and Vine holding back the wall and roof of the tunnel until the miners could escape.

Creatures as unsubstantial as ghosts normally would not be expected to hold back tons of rock and dirt. Yet there were many instances in which the weight of a ghost was remarkably more than the air he was made of. Mr. Conice, a Central City miner in 1868, was working in the Saratoga Mine when some ethereal visitors dropped in on him. The first was an ordinary mining spook minus his head. The headless gentleman greeted Conice politely and with his permission introduced a spectral companion who was exceedingly fat. If he had been flesh and blood, according to Conice, he "could have easily taken the grand prize at a hog show." Conice returned pleasantries, inviting the spooks to share his lunch. Agreeing, the three started up the ladder. Why the ghosts did not simply float up the shaft, as was their wont, is a curiosity, unless the fat one feared he could not get airborne. When Conice was on the upper part of the ladder, the fat ghost hastily stepped on the same rung, breaking it and sending the miner to the bottom. Conice was recovered by fellow miners with a few of his bones broken, vowing he would never trust a fat ghost again.

Other miners not only trusted in their private specters but followed their instructions. J.C. Dunn and William Quinn, who discovered the Highland Mary in 1873 near Silverton, said they were directed to the spot by a benign spirit. Another miner, in the Osceola Mine at Ophir, insured his safety by faithfully obeying directions from the shade of his deceased grandmother.

The majority of mining men were unafraid of the supernatural beings they worked with in the dim, cool mines. The Tommyknockers were, of course, the favorites. In all the mines (except the Mamie R.) the Tommyknockers, a breed of elfin men, protected the miners with unswerving charity. From time to time, however, these sprites enjoyed good-humored mischief, as did many of the ghosts.

Mining ghosts were usually a jolly crew fond of practical jokes. A favorite prank was to signal the engineer, after all the men had come up, that a miner was left below. The required search got under way, then peals of laughter bounced around and down the shafts as the specter eluded the searchers. In the Mikado Mine at Leadville similar nonsense on the part of the resident ghost occurred on a monthly basis. This spirit flitted from level to level as fancy suited him, and he enjoyed signalling the engineer at one station, then immediately at another. Some said he was the ghost of a miner who swore to W.C. Chadbourne, the property manager, that he would haunt him. Chadbourne had earlier ordered the miner and a partner to work the "Black Stope," a dangerous section with an evil history. They protested. The first said he would return to haunt if he were killed. Killed they both were, and a night shortly after their deaths, the one came up behind Chadbourne and tapped him on the shoulder. "Well, Chad," said the spirit, "I told you I'd haunt you, and here I am." He let out a roar of laughter and went echoing away like a loon through the workings, greatly distressing the guilt-ridden manager.

Miners probably would have been a miserable lot without their Tommyknockers, ghosts, and wraiths. The creatures were an integral part of their profession, a sort of sunlight where none ever shone. The men always kept a place for their spooks at the bar on Saturdays, and they fondly remembered them to their children at the home fireside. Newspapers of the day gave ample space to these supernatural visitors whenever one got up extra energy deep in the mountainside or at the mill, and if anyone ever suggested to a miner he was the victim of his own imagination, his only reply would be an expression that transcended words.

As Colorado's grand era of gold and silver faded, the mine ghosts seemed to go with it. They had blossomed in a queer light all their own. Then, as the icy winds of technology began to blow, the blossoms withered one by one, petals scattered over an uncompromising, unbelieving new generation.

And yet the abandoned mines and mills of that age, crumbling on secluded cliffs or tucked into narrow valleys, suggest that their blackened hollows may still be occupied by a stray ghost or a dozen stubborn Tommyknockers. When wandering down the cavernous throat of a lifeless mine, one may never know what eyes are watching. The cold air, the flat echoes, the low sighs, and the plip-plip of water are suggestive of spirit inhabitation, a melancholy longing, perhaps, for the miners who toiled within to return and rouse the place with that old familiar sound of blasting, tramming, and plain hard work. Ghosts, in general, are lonesome creatures. They tarry in these spots, where once they were surrounded by the noise of living comrades, simply for the memory of vanished happiness, waiting for the tender touch of the past to return.

Clinging to one of the loneliest places in Colorado is a forlorn child of yesterday. She must have been extremely happy once, her days filled with men and women and fuzzy-nosed burros whom she loved with all the passion of her young heart. Now she walks alone in the twilight of late autumn or winter days among the ruins of the North London Mill. Every sagging gray board and the delicate pattern of the wallpaper in an empty house nearby seem to be etched with this child's energy of love, yet somehow a quiet, lost love that falls upon nothing more than slivers, rusted cables, and powdery bricks.

The deserted North London Mill sleeps on the knees of Mosquito Pass at 11,500 feet. In its spring it was a veritable beehive of activity. Its lofty four stories at present are occupied by wind or ice, mouse or marmot, as it falters in its humble old age before the ravaging winters. The mill is empty and dreamless, with gaping wounds of twisted tin and stained beams still holding stairsteps that lead to nowhere. Yet, as if the miners had brought her there as they brought their favorite phantoms of old, the small child comes in the evening when there is a hush over the valley. She arrives from nowhere. Perhaps she is always there. She leaves no footprints. Wandering through the listing houses and on through the mill, she gaily calls men by name to come hither and sing with her. She seeks them out floor by floor, corner by corner as if replaying an old game. But there is no one to sing with her, and she abandons her search, sitting on a topmost beam in the mill, singing softly to herself. Her tiny voice is the only sound in the valley, except a low humming in the wind.

Or is that low sound the voice of many miners coming to sing with her, coming out of the jeweled twilight...coming home? Do they return and tell her tales of the sparkling, impetuous long ago when men were never too small to dream? Do they tell the beloved child about Tommyknockers or thieving goblins or mischievous spirits or any of those countless other sprites and phantoms they treasured?

They must! They must, for as night closes upon the North London Mill there is the sound of soft laughter and the clapping of little hands.

CHAPTER XI

Sticks and Bones

he huge, extraordinary Indian chieftain stood in the doorway of Charlie Barnsford's room, looking rather peaked. This Indian had been dead several hundred or perhaps a thousand years. Charlie, who had been sleeping, awoke in fright, forgetting the hospitality of the West, and told the apparition to take his "hoss to another pasture." Actually, Charlie was too scared to say those words; he only thought them as he leaped over to Joe DeRemer's bed to wake him.

When Joe snarled into consciousness, the ghost was gone. Joe had a mind to make Charlie gone also, but the terrified young Mr. Barnsford insisted there had been an Indian ghost beckoning at the door.

"He was a giant," explained Charlie. "His face was white, and he wore a white buckskin costume different from anything I've ever seen."

"Unn-huh," yawned Joe. "Well, Charlie, should he come back, invite him in for a smoke."

The following day Charlie Barnsford and his father, who owned a ranch near Trinidad, discovered the reason for the ghost chief's visit. Their neighbor, Juan Vasquez, who lived a half-mile west, had disturbed an ancient graveyard when he was digging the foundation for a new house. He had found the first of the bones the previous morning, releasing or angering the spirits. The bones and skulls of the dead were said to be nearly twice the size of those of modern Indians. The Barnsfords and Vasquez found them exceedingly interesting and took several specimens to Dr. Beshoar in Trinidad.

Soon anthropologists and other connoisseurs of the art of bone picking dropped upon Vasquez's foundation hole. They were tumbling over themselves with excitement in that autumn of 1870, believing they had come upon evidence of a race of giants. The Indians and Mexicans in the vicinity knew of no graveyard there; thus, the bone pickers concluded the graveyard was indeed ancient.

"It is quite ancient," said Professor Le Os, writing the date "1756" on a piece of paper.

"Oh yes, yes," agreed Dr. Knochen, scrawling "about the time of Constantine the Great" in his notebook.

"Ancient," pronounced Dr. Hueso, scribbling the notation "40,000 years" in his field book.

Anthropology was not yet a particularly advanced science, especially in the West, where most anthropologists were actually undertakers, dentists, or carpenters. They greedily collected the bones from the Vasquez site, even though when the remains were exposed to the air they disintegrated. But doctors knew how to set broken bones, so every fragmented tooth and fractured clavicle was numbered and bagged.

As was commonly the case when graveyards were disturbed, the related spirits slipped out of the rock, the dirt, and the blue to protest. For several weeks, while the hysterical ancient-history buffs groveled in the hole, the hysterical ancient-history spooks went calling around the neighborhood, frightening everyone except a Trinidad attorney.

A young Mexican woman residing two miles up the creek from the Barnsford ranch was the second victim to elicit the attention of the angry spirits. One night, when the woman's husband was out with the sheep, there came several thunderous knocks on the roof of her house. Knowing the usual place for polite society to knock was on the door, the woman knew whoever wanted to come in at the roof was either mad, unfriendly, or both. She sent her protector, an old retired sheepdog, to investigate. Ambling out the door, the dog yawned in the cool air, stretched, and curled up on the porch. When the roof-pounding again resounded, the woman had only one alternative: prayer. She fell to her knees, praying for deliverance, and at that moment the giant chief appeared before the lady.

He was dazzlingly white, terrifying, and above all, big. Although he had the features of an Indian, the spirit's face was as white as his clothing. The sheepherder's wife gave him no chance for conversation. She rushed out of her house and ran the two miles to Barnsford's house.

By the end of the week the ancient Indian's ghost was terrorizing everyone from Juan Vasquez to the sheepherders out in the sage. The uncivilized spirit blew over sheepherders' wagons and pounded and thumped on ranchers' walls, roofs, and occasionally doors. Barnsford's house was thumped upon many nights consecutively, and one of his visitors, H.S. Strickler, was even thumped. Strickler, hearing the strange noises overhead, went outside, procured a ladder, climbed up to the roof to see who was doing the pounding, and was thumped in the ear with a stick. He fell off the roof. One of the anthropologists was summoned to put Strickler back together again.

After several weeks of these disturbances, a news reporter in company with W.G. Rifenburg of Trinidad and Mr. Boyles, the unflinching attorney, visited the Barnsford ranch, which had become the central haunt of the angry spooks, possibly because the anthropologists roomed there.

The men were gathered around a blazing fire in the parlor, exchanging the latest judge and jury jokes, hotel jokes, and ghost jokes when the roof-knocking commenced. There was a thunderous thump-thump-thump quickly followed by a gentler knock-knock-knock.

"Who's there?" said Boyles, taking a long draw on his cigar.

The thumps came harder.

"Well, let them in, Barnsford," said Boyles. "It is a cold night."

"They could come in if they wished to," replied the rancher. "Walls never stopped them before."

The noise had ceased, and the rancher's twenty-year-old son related his encounter with the spirit...for the tenth time that evening. Oddly, no one exhibited tendencies to nod off or to stare blankly at their boottips. Suddenly, two sticks of wood in the fire began to dance, swaying from side to side, until one of them went flying up the chimney.

The men rushed outside to see if the stick was still airborne. They found it thirty yards from the house burning as brightly as if it were yet in the fireplace. Since the stick had made its curious departure without noise or explosion or smell of sulfur, the ranchers and company stood about staring at it until the cold wind blew some sense into them and they returned shivering to the house. Around the fire again, they discoursed on the recent phenomenon as intelligently as was possible under the circumstances. To what lengths could a rancher, lawyer, hotel proprietor, and newsman stretch their intellects on the subject of dancing, flying sticks? Newsmen were stretched from birth in the area of cerebral fiber; thus, that gentleman got on famously. Eventually, this exciting business ended for the evening, and the reporter dispatched a detailed narrative, resulting in a deluge of curiosity seekers to Barnsford's ranch, a few professed spiritualists among them.

There were additional thumpings to delight and terrify observers, there were a few more stick ballets, and several people swore they saw the giant Indian spirits. One gentleman claimed he saw a matched pair, with whom he shared a ceremony of pipe smoking, the pipe an ancient specimen supplied by the ghosts. At the conclusion, the spirits presented the man with the sacred pipe, which he guarded jealously. When Boyles saw it, he remarked that the pipe "appeared neither ancient nor ghostly" and suggested that the man had been smoking a length of hemp to produce his fantasy. Other witnesses told equally wild tales of the Indian spirits. Then abruptly the hauntings ceased. Were the spirits appeased? Did Juan Vasquez give them burnt offerings?

The anthropologists and other assorted men of science had left the site, carting away armfuls of bones. The ghosts weren't exactly gone: they had followed the anthropologists to their musty offices. After all, it was with them that the spirits had a bone to pick.

CHAPTER XII

The Last Man Who Spat on the Floor

pittoons were in railway cars. Spittoons were in saloons. Spittoons were in hotel lobbies, barbershops, and depots. Yet men still spat on the floor. "Disgusting! Uncivilized!" said Frank Pierce as he tossed up his hands in frustration. "Everywhere one walks there is spit, spit, spit!"

The hems of ladies' dresses trailed in it. Little children slipped in it. It got on the bottom of countless shoes and was transported everywhere, staining, soiling, sliming, and contaminating the city of Denver. Frank Pierce wasn't going to let it slide by any longer.

Pierce was a telegraph operator at the old Denver depot in 1871. This early, two-story brick building at the foot of Twenty-second Street had none of the pretentious echoing rooms, arches, clock tower, or gardens of the grand Union Depot built in 1880, but it was a respectable place where men ought not to have indulged in the barbaric practice of spitting on the floor. Spitting of any sort was a barbaric practice in the delicate opinion of Frank Pierce, who undoubtedly carried out all his expectorating in the privacy of his privy.

The first serious blunder at the railway depot was to strategically locate cuspidors about the place. Quite naturally, these brass fixtures proclaimed, in their gaping fashion, that a man was welcome to spit. Alas, the flood gates were opened. Men spat...and missed. Soon men became unconcerned with aim, due to the muddle on the floor in the general vicinity of the spittoons, and spat wherever the notion scratched them.

Let a cuspidor into life and civilization is through! Every place of business slips along on slimy, grimy, filthy goo!

Thus it came to pass that in 1871 Frank Pierce, late of Iowa, waged a discreet battle against the offensive expectorators at the Denver Depot.

Although described by his contemporaries as a "wild and mischievous fellow," Pierce began innocently enough. With extreme courtesy, he requested that gentlemen would graciously spit (if spitting could be done graciously) into the cuspidors and NOT UPON THE FLOOR. Thank you, sirs.

When the polite request was ignored, Pierce put up signs that asked, "Please do not spit upon the floor." He reserved his gratitude only for actual obedience. His bold signs went unheeded. More effective measures had to be employed.

One night Pierce procured a skull from the old potter's field in west Denver. He polished it, wired up the lower jaw, and hung the skull on his office wall with a placard beneath that read, "The last man who spat on the floor."

In the morning, when the grinning skull was observed by the expectant expectorators, they quietly took their juice-filled cheeks outdoors. But the skull produced an even greater impression on the night agent.

Alone in the office after dark with only the silent telegraph receiver and the unsalivating skull for company, the night agent soon heard queer sounds—slurred hollow speech—coming from the skull. A cold blast of air scattered the papers on his desk. Courageously, he sneered at the "last man who spat on the floor" and entertained methods of vengeance on Frank Pierce, certain Pierce was playing a trick.

Naturally, Pierce denied any trickery the following morning. When asked by the night agent if he would please remove the skull, Pierce assured him the skull was there to stay. It was the only effective means to keep the floors clean. There were mops, muttered the night agent as he left, realizing that the skull would remain as long as Frank Pierce remained.

Throughout each day all was well. No one spat on the floor, and the skull was silent. But at night...

The night agent soon resigned his situation, claiming he was disturbed by a constant draft and supernatural sounds. Passersby on the street and a few night travelers also heard the moaning and whispering noises at the depot. One night a dog was drawn to the door, where he remained to howl till dawn. Even Pierce braved the dark hours to observe the complaining skull and concluded it merely wanted a hat. He immediately supplied the boney fellow with a hunting cap. There the skull hung, grinning on the wall with a floppy plaid cap covering its yellowed forehead. It should have been happy. But night agents and telegraph operators fled or resigned, leaving Pierce to discover why the skull yet complained. Perhaps it wanted a cigar.

Pierce clamped a cigar between the jaws of the skull, telling it this was the last thing he would bother to supply it. No more complaints.

About this time a few railroad employees claimed a "cadaverous,

weird, and emaciated" man rose up out of the mound from which
Frank Pierce had removed the skull, walked along the street to a corral,
on to a saloon, and then prowled around the perimeter of the Denver
Depot, peering in at the windows. The moaning sound came when
the apparition was near Pierce's office. The employees believed the
spirit belonged to the skull, or vice versa, and wanted the stolen
cranium returned.

For many a month Pierce worked undisturbed with the grinning,
cigar-smoking skull staring down from his wall. He had no intention
of removing it, though others urged him to do so. When he finally
left the city for other prospects, the telegraph operator who replaced
him thought the skull rather amusing until he heard the terrible moaning
and felt the chilling air in the office and saw a faint haggard face
staring at him through the window. The skull was reburied. The
disturbing noises ceased. But for some reason the ragged ghost continued to haunt the place.

Ticket agents and telegraph operators could not be encouraged to
keep their employment at the depot once they encountered the apparition. The barely visible tramp with a strange expression was seen
often looking in at the windows. Sometimes the figure raised a yellowed
hand bearing only three fingers and tapped on the glass. He would
hoarsely call the agent within by name. Displaying a crooked grin
remarkably like that of the celebrated skull, the vaporous tramp would
wave his mutilated hand and vanish, only to appear at the inside
door or the ticket window.

One frosty night, the apparition was observed standing on the
depot landing as if waiting for a train. When a switchman chased the
creature away with a swinging lantern and a good deal of hollering,
the ghost disappeared into the woodwork. In a moment he reappeared
in Frank Pierce's old office, asking for a ticket to Omaha. He scared
the unmentionables off the night agent, who resigned the next morning.
For nearly ten years the tramp thus occupied himself, always appearing
between 1:00 and 2:00 A.M., the hour when Frank Pierce was said to
have first disturbed the grave. The spirit didn't confine himself to the
depot, but took a trot around the neighborhood, stopping occasionally at a nearby saloon.

Finally, the railway company tore down the building to make way
for the new Union Depot and train yards. Despite the construction
of this new building, rumor had it that the old station was abandoned because the ghost drove away so many agents and telegraph
operators. When the old station was demolished, the ghost seemed to

vanish beneath the rubble. He was seen no more in the neighborhood or at the saloon. He was no longer observed rising from the burial site.

For a brief time in the early 1930s, a very faint, washed-out shade was seen on a rare night wandering through the walls of Union Station. The few persons, as rare as the nights, who observed the apparition said it drifted about aimlessly, poking in at this door and that. Then it faded into the long shadows between decades.

Again, at present, there is mention of a ghost who haunts the Union Depot. The building, diminished in size and grandeur, echoes with a certain melancholy sound, like an old spinster aunt thinking dreamily on her days of glorious youth, when there were crowds of passengers, countless steaming trains, Pullman cars, elegant dining halls, and those polished brass cuspidors. Technology and civilization have taken the steam out of rail travel and the spit out of the shine. But the ghost, like the depot, seems to long for those wild days.

The Spirit of the Depot Present has only been sensed, not seen, and employees have christened him the "Soldier" or the "Lieutenant," perhaps mistakenly. Could it be the last man who spat on the floor has returned, looking for an old familiar face, or hat, or. . .spittoon?

CHAPTER XIII

Death Cry

f Christian C. Brisbane and his wife, Anne, had been informed that they had been selected to have their hair raised and their skin set to crawling, they doubtless would have remained home that blustery day. But since the selection committee related to hair-raising events are a secretive lot, Mr. and Mrs. Brisbane merrily set out from their farm south of Denver.

As the couple traveled south in their rattling buggy toward Franktown, ominous thunderheads billowed up in the northern sky, rumbling obscene threats to summer travelers. The more faith the Brisbanes manifested that they would reach their destination before the storm let loose, the more savage was the wind, hurling grit into their faces and causing their horse to balk. With a great flash of lightning, the rain came in a deluge, and Mr. and Mrs. Brisbane were forced to shelter their wet faith in a deserted cabin close at hand.

The cabin, smelling of fragrant organic compost and rodent habitation, crouched in Coyote Gulch, a short distance from Bayou Gulch. The large log front room and two smaller frame rooms at the rear had been unoccupied for several years, the old homey atmosphere deteriorating with the woodwork. Rain poured in through the cracks in the walls and roof, and wind tore at the door and wailed at the windows. Thinking the place rather quaint and cozy, the Brisbanes decided they would stay the night, since the torrential downpour showed no sign of letting up. They had brought a picnic lunch and blanket with them, which would suffice for their short visit.

As night closed in with wind and rain still lashing the place with a fury, Christian started a fire in the dilapidated fireplace, hoping no birds had stuffed nests in the chimney. He and Anne sat before the cheery blaze, singing ditties and gaily chatting. With crumbs they enticed a tiny, shy fieldmouse out of his corner and made him scamper quickly into the shadows with their laughter. Suddenly, their revelry was shattered by a terrible cry of mortal agony resounding from the small room overhead.

Anne's face lost all color. Christian held his breath and looked at the ceiling as if he possessed the power of seeing through solid objects. Although the sound was as distinct a scream as ever issued from the human lungs, Christian said, "It is only a mouse, my dear," hoping to spare his wife the horror of thinking that a raving lunatic was lodged above. He arose quietly and started toward the narrow staircase, which was little more than a ladder with flat rungs.

"No!" cried his wife in a whisper. "What if some horrid thing is up there?"

"If there is," replied Christian, "it may come down here."

Anne clung to her husband, pleading for him to stay with her or to take her upstairs with him; in any event not to leave her alone. He told her to remain where she was. He took a large, burning stick from the fire and disappeared up the steps. Christian's footsteps made no noise overhead, and Anne, waiting like a ghost before the fire, found the desolation of the howling wind and driving rain unbearable.

"Christian?" she called after an eternity of two or three minutes. "Chistian? Christian!"

Hearing no answer from her husband, Anne panicked, believing instantly that he was "done in." She called his name frantically, the tears streaming down her cheeks. Only the howling wind answered. Christian was dead, she was certain, and she was left alone to await the same awful fate in this awful cabin in this awful gulch. Of course, she could be mistaken; she had heard no noise of a body falling. With this snatch of hope, Anne slowly crept upstairs. Christian was not there.

An old weathered bedstead slumped in the shadowed far corner like a crude sarcophagus. The bed and floor were littered with trash, leaves, and rodent dung. A window without glass, where the tortured wraith of a curtain twisted in the wind, overlooked the roof of the cabin's back rooms. Anne could hear the pounding of her heart as she moved to the window and peered out. At that moment another agonized cry split the night, a cry in the very room where Anne stood. But the terrified woman didn't stand any longer. Her legs buckled and she slid down the wall shaking violently, crying and tormented by the vision of her husband lying bleeding in the rain somewhere.

Desperate and blinded by tears, Anne forced herself to go back down the stairs. When she reached the front room, the tall, black figure of a man burst in the door. Anne screamed as Christian caught her in his arms.

With the consolation of kisses and hugs, Christian assured his wife he was no bogey beast. He explained that when he had gone upstairs he thought he saw a man go out the window; thus, he went out also, climbing down the lower roof. But he found no one near the place, nor did he see any footprints in the mud. When he heard the second cry he decided it came from an owl...an owl with a hearty set of vocal chords...so he returned to the cabin.

"Screech owls sometimes make a terrible cry," said Christian. "I'm sure that is all we heard, and probably when I went upstairs I frightened it out the window."

No owl, no mouse, no creature great or small made that cry, Anne told her well-intentioned husband. She had suddenly realized that the cry was from a dead man, a murdered dead man, and she wasn't staying in this awful cabin a minute longer. In fact, as she spoke she packed the basket. But what about the rain? Go out in the storm, dear? Court pneumonia, dear? It was only an owl, dear, not a dead man. Every rational woman knew dead men didn't scream. There was no rationalizing to be done in this case; dead men do scream, Anne assured her husband, and she was leaving, pneumonia or otherwise. She had realized that the cabin was the infamous McIntyre cabin, where one man was brutally slain and others were suspected to have met their ends.

The name McIntyre was enough to rekindle Christian's damp memory. He abandoned the screaming mice and screeching owl theory in an instant, hurried with his wife to their soaking buggy and drowning horse, and rattled off to Franktown.

For over a decade, travelers said they heard the scream resound in Coyote Gulch on wild and stormy summer nights. Ranchers and farmers avoided the place, and everyone who knew of the murder said the cabin was haunted.

In 1871 the McIntyre family had taken up residence in the cabin, engaging other men's cattle in their own cattle business. The family consisted of a man and his two grown sons, Jack and Jim, and the man's second wife and her two children from a previous marriage. Besides being suspected of rustling, the family had a dubious reputation on all other counts. Travelers aware of that usually avoided their hospitality.

One night in June of 1873, a man from Denver, who had inadvertently allowed the stage to forget him at Twenty Mile House station, decided to walk the ten miles to the next stop, intending to procure a horse or catch the morning stage. The next stop was a small hotel at Russellville on the Denver to Pueblo stage line. Enroute to Russellville, the man was overtaken by a thunderstorm and sought shelter at the McIntyre house. About this time he was probably chiding himself for not taking the Denver & Rio Grande Railroad to Pueblo. Sometimes it was fatal to be too attached to stage travel.

The stranger was welcomed by Mr. McIntyre and sons, whose keen eyes scanned his fine wet suit of clothes and whose keen minds immediately set to work. He was given a hearty meal of rustled beef and offered a bed for the night. The stranger gratefully accepted and was shown to the room upstairs.

Late in the night when all was quiet, Jack and Jim McIntyre crept onto the back roof and through the window to where the stranger was dreaming peacefully of the hospitable ranchers of the West. The hospitable rancher's sons lost no time in thrusting a knife into the sleeping man, but the blow was not instantly fatal. The man let out a terrible cry of agony, which others living farther up the gulch heard. He struggled to fight off his assailants, but Jack delivered another thrust of the blade, killing the man. The brothers searched his pockets and found a large amount of cash, a small pouch of gold dust, the man's gold watch, and other personal effects. They then dragged the bleeding body out the window and down the roof. In an oak thicket at the rear of the house the man was buried in a shallow grave.

Early in the morning a few days later, about twenty armed men surrounded the house, demanding that the McIntyres come forth. The father and his sons were held under guard while the house was searched. Bloodstains were found on the upstairs bed and on the window sill. In a short time the body of the murdered man was unearthed.

Meanwhile, Jack McIntyre slipped past the guards and was never seen again. Enraged by the murder and Jack's escape, the party of men elected to hold court beneath a nearby pine, Honorable Judge Hemp presiding. Mrs. McIntyre pleaded for the life of her husband while ropes were fitted around his and Jim's necks. The two were given a moment for final confession, though absolution was not promised. Jim took the opportunity to rankle the jury by reciting the details of the murder with cold-blooded delight, pointing out his father's innocence in the undertaking. Men of reason and compassion, the jury let the old man go free, provided he and his wife and her children never again set foot in the territory. Jim, of course, was hanged, satisfying the prosecution and defense. Court was adjourned, and the body was buried at the foot of the pine.

After the McIntyres departed by the various techniques offered them, the cabin in Coyote Gulch was never again prime real estate. Travelers avoided it. Ranchers avoided it. Mr. and Mrs. Brisbane avoided it once they knew its defect. Even cattle avoided it, for neither man nor animal desired to have their rainstorms ruined by a terrible death cry.

CHAPTER XIV

One Sunday In September

he evening was fast dwindling into simpering smalltalk and dissertations on rare subjects by rarer guests at General Palmer's Glen Eyrie, when Charles Cavender and Brighton Haywood decided to indulge in the scented shadows of the garden. As the pair was strolling across the lawn, the figure of a man standing beneath the red rock spires caught Haywood's eye. Haywood stopped, a smile of recognition lighting his face.

"Why, that's young Schlesinger," he said, moving toward the figure.

Cavender restrained him by the arm as he muttered in alarm, "Impossible! That's impossible, Bright!"

"What is wrong?" replied Haywood. He couldn't understand the bewildered expression on his friend's face. "It's only young Schlesinger, is it not?"

Cavender shook his head, keeping a hand on Haywood. He was ill at ease as he glanced again at the motionless figure several yards away. The young man's pained eyes met his. Cavender drew in a sharp breath.

"It is impossible," he whispered.

"Don't be so blame mysterious," said Brighton Haywood. He went toward the shadowed man, but the man disappeared behind the rocks and could not be found.

"Look at you!" chuckled Haywood when he returned to the statuary that once was Charles Cavender. "Perhaps you and Schlesinger have had too much of the general's Madeira, judging by your peculiar behavior."

"That wasn't Arthur Schlesinger," said Cavender, staring blankly at the rocks. He shook his head and turned to Haywood. "Arthur was killed months ago. Dead, Bright. That was not him."

Haywood laughed. "A good joke," he said, "but a bit macabre."

"No, no," replied Charles. "I swear it! Arthur was killed."

"But I saw him in my room a few nights ago," returned the other. "He stepped in briefly and left without speaking to me. I suppose he thought I was asleep. If he is dead, what the deuce is he doing here?"

Cavender turned away, tossing up his hands in supreme confusion.

"It was someone else," he mumbled and went into the house.

Some weeks later an English maid was polishing the silver in Dr. William Bell's dining room when she was startled by a man's unannounced appearance in the corner of the room. The woman suddenly became as stiff as her starched dress. She carefully sidled toward the door, keeping her eyes on the strangely silent intruder. Just as she reached the doorway, a young governess was passing by, and the maid snatched her by the sleeve, drawing her into the room.

"A ghost!" whispered the maid, still eyeing the man.

"Arthur Schlesinger!" gasped the governess. She sank against the starched servant, aghast. At that moment the vision vanished into the woodwork.

Rumors began to drift around Colorado Springs that the young European-born gentleman had slipped the bonds of his grave. Friends and acquaintances caught sight of his sorrowful ghost at Glen Eyrie and Queen's Canyon, at Dr. Bell's house and at Dr. Solly's cottage. Strolling sweethearts saw him by moonlight as a tragic shadow in the Garden of the Gods, and others said he loitered at Crow's Roost outside of town.

Arthur J.L. Schlesinger had come to Colorado Springs in January of 1876. He was hired as a secretary in the Denver & Rio Grande Railroad offices of General William Jackson Palmer and as Dr. Samuel Edwin Solly's private secretary, rooming at Dr. Solly's house. He was a dashing, pleasant young man with a quiet attraction for the reckless side of life. Although he was as fine a shot as a blind skunk, Arthur enjoyed target shooting and hunting with his friends.

Arthur's closest friend was the flamboyant British physician, Dr. Solly, who promoted the springs at Manitou with a pamphlet ascribing marvelous healing powers to the water, powers modern medicine could never duplicate. The doctor was also instrumental in enticing the diamond-encrusted peers of England to the little colony below Pikes Peak. Being a member of Colorado Springs's loftiest society, Dr. Solly became young Schlesinger's ticket to hobnob with the sparkling upper crust. He was often invited to dazzling dinners and parties at General Palmer's, Dr. Bell's, Madame Hamp's, Mr. Connell's, and others. Arthur spent many days riding the general's fine horses at Glen Eyrie and many nights as practically a member of the household. He kept company with Hanson A. Risley, General Palmer's lawyer, learning the finer arts of evading the flock of young ladies who seemed intent on bagging him as a wall trophy. Although he adored these fluttering flowers, he never seriously courted any one of them.

By summer Arthur had become a popular gentleman of society. He was invited on picnic hikes to Jones Park and Lake Moraine. He indulged in horse racing and midnight dancing. He led the life of an enraptured bee, tripping from flower to flower in dizzy delight.

One day Arthur confided in Hanson Risley that he had had a duel with his English tutor, Mr. Stanton, while in France. The duel was over a young lady who Schlesinger said traveled with him later to New York, but whom he had not seen since. The tutor, whom Arthur only wounded, said he would find him some day and have his revenge.

A slightly altered version of the tale was told to Dr. Solly. Arthur related to the physician that he had killed Stanton in the duel and felt unhappy about it. He also lamented his reckless past of gambling, foolish extravagance, and infidelity to his family. Dr. Solly gave the story little thought until Sunday, 10 September 1876.

Sunday morning, before Arthur Schlesinger left Dr. Solly's house, he asked the doctor to please collect his mail at the post office that afternoon, as he was expecting an important letter from France. Arthur, who was leaving on the train for Pueblo, asked Dr. Solly to open the letter and telegraph him the news.

"He didn't state the nature of the news," said Dr. Solly, "only that I was to telegraph. Nor did he tell me the object of his trip to Pueblo.

"I waited for the mail, which was not delivered until after five o'clock, when I found no letters for Mr. Schlesinger, but two for myself, from him."

The first letter apologized for the pretense. The second stated that Arthur had agreed to a duel at noon that day, but expected to fail. If he did not return to town by four-thirty, he wished Dr. Solly to send out to Lawson's ranch for his body.

Dr. Solly, unflappable Englishman that he was, was stunned. He searched the young man's room for any clue, any letter which might reveal the name of the challenger. He found nothing. Hurrying over to Hanson Risley's house, he showed the letters to the attorney. The two procured a carriage and drove out to Lawson's ranch, reaching the place around ten o'clock Sunday night.

The ranch house was deserted. All was silent. Dr. Solly and Mr. Risley called out for Arthur and searched to no avail. Finally, when the moon rose, shedding more light on the scene, Arthur's body was discovered in a sandy gulch 150 yards from the house. He was lying on his face with his right arm beneath his head, a lady's white handkerchief beside him, his gun a few yards in front, and a bullet hole in his right breast. The body had fallen across a line drawn in the sand.

When the coroner, R.T. Taylor, went out to the corpse early the next morning, an examination of the area revealed another line drawn in the sand twenty paces from the body, where there were faint footprints. Two spent shells were in Schlesinger's revolver. Two others were in the sand near the opposite line. There were several horse and carriage tracks leading from the spot to the road.

Arthur Schlesinger's cold body was taken into town, and for three days the coroner's jury attempted to discover whether the young gentleman had been murdered, shot in a duel, or committed suicide. Numerous witnesses were called and recalled. Friends, businessmen, and a sheepherder were questioned. Had Schlesinger quarreled with anyone? Had he been despondent? Had he mentioned any peculiar circumstances? No, no, no. Up to the time of his death all had appeared normal.

The Sunday before Arthur's demise, he and John Wilson had gone out to the latter's ranch, about thirty miles southeast of town. The two stopped on the way at Lawson's ranch for water. They met Messrs. Summers, Wheeler, Sutton, and Barnes there and exchanged friendly horse talk. Then they continued on. Arthur stayed at Wilson's ranch until Wednesday morning, target shooting and rabbit shooting, both of which he did poorly. He also ran his horse as if preparing for a race. Wilson told the coroner's jury that Arthur was in cheerful spirits, no different than his usual self.

When Dr. Jacob Reed, who performed the postmortem, first testified, he said he believed the "deceased did not fire the shot." He found no powder burn, and the angle of the ball's path through Arthur's body indicated that the ball was fired from a height of five and a half to six feet, the height of a man holding a revolver at arm's length. Curiously, Dr. Reed changed his testimony the next day, claiming that he did find a burn and that the "condition of the liver would carry the influence that the pistol was held in contact with the body." Dr. Henry K. Palmer, who assisted in the postmortem, disagreed. He said there was no powder burn. Likewise, Coroner Taylor could see no burn upon examining the clothing of the deceased.

Despite this and further testimony through Wednesday, five members of the coroner's jury delivered a verdict of suicide, while the remaining member was adamant that "the deceased came to his death by a pistol shot fired by a person or persons unknown."

Colorado Springs, shocked by Arthur's death, was outraged by the verdict of suicide.

"He was a young man of character and promise," said Dr. Solly.

"He would do no such thing!" Charles Cavender angrily stated. "He never even hinted at such a thing."

"He was a man of honor and high spirit," added Hanson Risley, "not likely to carry out an elaborate scheme to make a suicide appear a duel."

Suicide carried a terrible stigma, and the people of Colorado Springs would not have it; they would not believe it. What man carefully planned his suicide a full week in advance? What victim of suicide traveled fifteen miles for the sole purpose of shooting himself? Were there not tracks at the scene? Were there not other spent cartridges? Were there not lines drawn in the sand as if for a duel? The editor of the *Gazette* reported that the majority of people in Colorado Springs believed Arthur's "tragical death was the sequel to some youthful indiscretion, if not something worse, in the foreign land from whence he came."

For months the Springs's citizens wondered about the terrible death in their happy city. They felt a sadness in their hearts for young Arthur, speaking of him in subdued tones. Perhaps it was their concern that brought his shadow to their houses, a shadow longing for the sunlight, longing for the touch of their warm hands.

In 1888 a Colorado Springs gentleman, who had lately returned from a visit to New York, related a curious tale one night at a society party. In New York, while he was dining as a guest of a wealthy English lady, the conversation turned to Colorado Springs, and someone mentioned the duel of Arthur Schlesinger. The Colorado Springs gentleman related the story of Arthur's death in 1876, causing the English lady to grow pale and agitated. She made her apologies and left the dinner table.

"After further inquiry I came to the conclusion Madam was the lady whom young Schlesinger had fought over," said the gentleman. "Later she took me aside, begging me not to reveal anything I might know of her past. I found it a strange request, but told her the honor of her name was secure with me."

The gentleman kept his word, and no clues to Arthur Schlesinger's mysterious death ever slipped out of the hazy corners of stone mansions. In time Arthur fell among the unremembered passions of youth, his faint melancholy ghost wandering at Briarhurst and Glen Eyrie, unrecognized except on those quaint, soft nights in late summer when the sweet, scented gardens invited lovers for a stroll.

"I cannot forget the night I saw poor Arthur's ghost," said one of the transplanted English ladies of Manitou. "Never, not ever shall I forget that profound sadness in his eyes."

CHAPTER XV

A Meadowlark's Shadow

loudless and brilliant blue, the late summer sky echoed a transcendent symphony of birdsong. Living music of cliff swallow, horned lark, magpie, and meadowlark mingled with laughter, excited conversation, and the arguing of mules around Glendale House. Nearby, shallow Beaver Creek slipped into cottonwood groves and out again to catch the sunlight on its clear water, casting a sparkle of diamonds from bank to bank.

The stage station of Glendale, with its handful of dwellings, was settled in 1861, and the hostelry was built by John McClure where the bloodred sand of Red Creek meets the silver slash of Beaver Creek, east of Penrose.

The forty-foot long, two-story Glendale House was constructed of native stone. Mortar made with the red sands of the creeks gave the house a pink sunset cast. Built on a small rise above Beaver Creek, the inn was surrounded by pasture lands and had a view of the distant blue mountains.

The eleven-bedroom stage house was never full unless there were more than four to a bed and no spare corners to unroll a blanket. It had two cozy parlors warmed by large fireplaces, and the rear wing contained a deep cellar and an ice room, small kitchen, and dining room.

A wide green lawn aproned the front entry, and several favorite black locust trees brought from the East were planted around the building, one by the well, where the fragrance of their spring blossoms freshened the mule-tainted air.

To the east and southeast of the inn were stables and corrals for scores of horses and mules. These animals outfitted stagecoaches enroute to the South Park gold fields and later silver caches. Behind Glendale House, down a few stone steps to creek level, was Glendale Garden, a favorite spot for visitors and neighbors.

This garden was an area of lush grass beneath the cottonwoods. Hedges of feathery pink tamarix and beds of sky-blue chicory, pansies, geraniums, snapdragons, and bachelor buttons brightened the spot. There were benches for sitting and dreaming while the Downy woodpecker hammered overhead and light and shadow played on Beaver Creek.

Just beyond this little garden paradise the vegetable garden thrived with healthy doses of mule plaster.

The homegrown vegetables, inspired cuisine of wild game and fowl, and the generous hospitality of Glendale House became well known to travelers. By 1877, when Leadville's silver boom had again brought hundreds of men to its doors, the house was also a popular place for social gatherings, Sunday picnics, celebrations, and weddings.

On a bright Sunday in late summer of that year, several families were enjoying a basket dinner in the garden. There was laughter and song while magpies guffawed high in the trees and meadowlarks piped from corral fences. A hint of autumn tinged the Virginia creeper on the hotel's walls copper and deep red. Pots of bright geraniums trimmed the front balcony, peeking between the balusters like curious children. Roasted venison, hot currant pies, apple pies, and fresh bread tempted many of the inn's lodgers to the picnic. By morning most of these men would be on their way to Leadville.

Kathleen Cooper, a rancher's daughter, strayed to the creek's edge to listen to an old scout play his mouth organ. She soon joined his song, singing sweetly.

One of the travelers who was due to leave on the morning stage heard Kathleen singing as he sat against a cottonwood. Rising to see what extraordinary bird belonged to the song, his gaze fell upon the blue-eyed, golden-haired girl.

"As beautiful as the meadowlark's song," said the stranger, startling Kathleen and the scout.

Kathleen blushed. The stranger was struck speechless, certain he beheld an angel. Apologizing, he identified himself as Julian LaSalle. Kathleen's friend graciously presented her.

In what seemed like no time at all, Julian was floating beside Kathleen among the picnickers. He met her father, her mother, her sisters, brothers, cousins, this farmer, and that rancher, all in a cloud lit by Kathleen. Everyone found Julian pleasant and good-humored. He was from Virginia and had journeyed west, searching for his own direction. In Santa Fe he had met an old friend who was heading for Leadville's riches. He had promised the friend he would join him in the autumn and assist in the venture. Now that his coach was leaving in the morning, there was a vague desire in him for the coach to turn into a bushel basket.

Julian was a tall, dashing, aristocratic gentleman. Reflected in his eyes was a depth of spirit and honesty that told Kathleen she had found the treasure no other human being could give. There in the twilight she knew she loved him from the tips of his dusty black boots to the top of his broadbrimmed hat, and she would love no other. She sang to him her meadowlark songs as darkness fell. Then her father called her out of her dream.

Kathleen reluctantly bade Julian goodnight and departed with her family in a carriage. That night Julian could not sleep. The morning stage would soon take him away and he feared he would never see Kathleen again.

Resolved to see her, Julian went to the Cooper ranch in the morning. One day's delay before heading to Leadville could not possibly make the sky fall down. He spent the extra day with Kathleen and her family until again he had to say goodnight, but not before he promised to see her again one day, if she would allow it.

The dawn arrived too soon in a flush of pink and gold, with the stage standing ready in front of Glendale House. Julian was swinging his baggage into the boot when he heard a sweet voice call his name. Kathleen was driving toward him in a chaise.

They embraced one another while stage passengers crowded into and onto the coach. Julian asked if Kathleen would write to him, saying he would write to her every day. He did not know how he could get along in Leadville, for with her alone he had suddenly felt complete. Someone yelled to him to hurry up or the stage would leave him there. He knew he must go; he had promised his friend. In earnest he asked Kathleen to be his wife. She said yes; they would be married when he returned in the spring.

A stolen kiss, a whispered promise, a tear and farewell, and he was gone. Kathleen could only think of spring.

Julian arrived in a wild, rough, energetic, clamorous Leadville. He traded his gentleman's attire for workman's clothes and labored beside his friend, John A. Hoblit, in the Kittie Mine, named for Kathleen. As he promised, he wrote to Kathleen each day through the autumn and winter and received her letters of love with delight.

Soon the cold winter gave way to the brilliance of spring, and Kathleen's wedding day approached. She received a last letter from Julian, who wrote with joy that he would be at Glendale House on the appointed day; nothing could keep him away. The wedding ceremony and festivities were to be at the hostlery, and everyone the Coopers knew was invited.

On the wedding day in May of 1878, the Glendale House balcony was draped with bright bows and garlands of wildflowers. An "orchestra" played in the parlor, and the wine flowed freely. Although Julian's arrival was a day late, the wedding ceremony was still planned for five o'clock.

Everyone was already celebrating when Kathleen walked down the stairs and out on the front lawn in her wedding gown of white damasse silk and brocaded satin. On the bride's right shoulder was a spray of pink geranium blossoms tied with satin ribbons. A long tulle veil, white gloves, and white slippers completed the ensemble.

Kathleen danced with her father and a few old beaus as the afternoon crawled by. When five o'clock came and Julian did not, Kathleen grew anxious. Those present tried to assure her the gentleman would soon be there.

At seven o'clock Kathleen went to the balcony to watch for her tardy groom. She tried to dispel the notion that some ill had befallen him. He had lamed his horse or stopped to help someone or got caught in a storm or. . .or. . .there were dozens of trifling things to delay a man.

Twilight fell and still Julian was missing. Some friends were sent to look for him while Kathleen waited on the balcony, the gentle breezes sporting with her veil, the moonlight on her white figure. Each time she heard the sound of hooves coming up the road from Beaver Creek she arose in joyful anticipation, calling out, "Julian!" But invariably it would be a strange traveler. Late into the night she waited and hoped, watching the road for her beloved.

Finally her mother convinced her to get some rest, telling her all would be well in the morning. But dawn broke in bright darkness. Meadowlarks heralded the golden sun, and riders came slowly up the road leading a horse. The bay bore the wounded body of its master, the cold, lifeless body of the generous-hearted Virginian. Julian LaSalle had been robbed and murdered on the South Park road, and his remains were flung in the weeds where the searchers found his horse standing over him.

Bewildered and anguished, Kathleen looked upon the pallid handsome face. She touched his cheek gently and turned away. Friends and family tried to comfort her, but she ran from them to the cottonwood grove, falling upon the grass. Julian, come back! Come back! Come back!

Julian LaSalle could never come back. He was buried, and in the days following Kathleen remained silent in her room at the family ranch. She refused food. She refused companionship. She could not be comforted.

The physician recommended Kathleen have a change of scenery.

Sent to live with an uncle and aunt in Canon City, she went about the house in a state of abstraction. She grew pale, avoiding visitors, her joyful nature subdued. In autumn she took to her bed, and within a few days she died. Though the doctor said she died of influenza, others said she died of a broken heart.

The Meadowlark's voice was still as they laid her to rest dressed in her wedding gown. People spoke of her in whispers, respectful of her terrible grief, hoping she was happy at last in her final slumber. Then they spoke of her no more. New oil discoveries, coal, silver, and the railroad war of the Arkansas River dominated conversations and consumed energies in the Canon City area. The reckless pace of men and women went on through the autumn and winter. Snow came and went, and spring, as faithful as dawn, colored the land with green.

As the railroads advanced through the Arkansas Valley and South Park, travelers to Glendale House dwindled to a cartful. The era of the stagecoach was giving way to the iron horse. Glendale was rarely crowded, the hostelry serving mainly cowboys or ranchers in the area or an occasional traveler.

A solitary horseback rider arrived one night in late spring of 1879 via the Beaver Creek road. He greeted the lady on the upper porch, dismounted, and went inside. There were a few men and women in the parlor and dining room.

The man asked the proprietor about the pretty bride on the balcony, but the proprietor shook his head. There was no bride at Glendale House.

Later that summer another lone rider came to the inn at night. He, too, mentioned the beautiful bride on the balcony. The proprietor could only mumble something about wishful thinking. These young sports were anxious to be married perhaps?

By July 1880, after the Denver & Rio Grande Railroad reached Leadville, Glendale House had many a quiet night and yawning day. Except when an unexpected traveler stopped in and asked about the bride on the balcony. A few romantically inclined local cowboys and some of Glendale's fifteen residents told these strangers that Glendale House had a ghost. They swore on a stack of oysters that they had witnessed the apparition with their own eyes. Even Glendale's postmaster, J.D. Curtis, claimed to have seen the ghost in 1883. Originally a skeptic, Curtis was converted by a late-night experience.

The apparition was much discussed the next day. If Curtis saw it, they said, there truly was a ghost. A cowboy, Arthur Kinney, said he had heard the bride speak. She seemed to appear with the tramping of horse's hooves along the Beaver Creek road. They christened her the "Ghost Bride of Glendale House."

The following summer, a lone traveler along Beaver Creek neared Glendale House as night fell. He saw its lights a few hundred yards away and hoped for a soft bed. He was unaccustomed to equestrian travel over long distances, but had a desire to visit some of the quaint places off the steam track, wandering about and writing his impressions in a journal. That day he had visited Greenlee Spring in Wild Horse Park, rambling west over White Butte, down into Pierce Gulch, and finally up Beaver Creek to Glendale. He was tired and depressed, hot and dry, and considering giving up the entire journal idea for something less demanding, such as studying the habits of hibernating toads. Yes, hibernating toads would be quite suitable, he mused while riding up to the hotel. Something in the dark caught his eye. He heard a name called out. Above on the balcony he saw a beautiful young bride looking down at him, a melancholy expression in her eyes. He was seized with envy of the lucky groom and pleasantly greeted the lady with a tip of his hat. He went into the hotel thinking he would rather write about brides.

The proprietor, D.S. Coffman, told the inquiring stranger that Glendale House had plenty of rooms. He had a choice. After much traveling, the stranger said, a bed was a bed; any room would suit weary Thomas Woodbury. Then he changed his mind. If he had a choice, why not take the room next to the bride.

"There's no bride here," replied Coffman.

"I saw her," said Woodbury. "I saw her on the balcony as plain as I see you."

A few people in the parlor overheard the conversation and could not resist questioning the visitor. Three cowboys, the cook, the wife of a resident, and a gentleman lodger crowded around him. They delighted in the description Woodbury furnished, for no one before had described the girl as anything other than a "bride." She was their private pet ghost, but they did not explain such to Woodbury in order not to color his perception.

"She was blonde, petite, with a white gown of satin and lace with flowers on the skirt. Very lovely," related Woodbury. "The dress had a very long train and she wore a long veil. Ah yes, and there were little flowers on her shoulder. And you tell me there is no bride here!" He laughed. "You really musn't expect me to believe that. I not only saw her, I also heard her speak."

"What did she say?" said a cowboy eagerly. "Could you tell what she said?"

The few who had heard the bride speak never could discern her word.

"Just as I rode up she said 'Julian' as if she thought I were this Julian," said Woodbury. He laughed again. "I assure you, I would be pleased to be Julian."

They were all staring at him, astounded, speechless, gaping.

"What—?" said Woodbury, nervously. "Did I say something wrong?"

"It's Kathleen!" whispered Coffman. "The ghost is Kathleen Cooper!"

"Ghost?" replied Woodbury.

"She's still waiting for Julian," said the cook.

In the parlor, Woodbury heard the story of Kathleen and Julian. Only a few residents of Glendale remembered them, and none had previously realized the ghost bride was Kathleen.

Despite the popularity of the ghost tale, not many people had actually seen the ghost, and several of those who had later convinced themselves they had not, saying all they saw was the white of a barn owl in flight. Barn owls were commonly mistaken for spirits. Some people traveled to Glendale House simply for a glimpse of the bride in the moonlight, but were disappointed, for she never appeared when expected. The children of local ranchers and farmers had spread stories that Glendale House was haunted by a host of ghosts down by the lonesome cottonwood glen. The cowboys, however, told of only one, and that was the pretty bride.

As the seasons fluttered away and years turned into decades, Glendale House became deserted. The mules and horses were gone. No more travelers stayed within her walls. No more men or women went up and down her narrow staircases. The gardens were choked with weeds, and the chicory and tamarix had escaped to grow like vagabonds along Beaver Creek and beneath the towering cottonwoods. The house appeared a perfect haunt for lost souls, and local tales lodged many spirits in its rooms. Cowboys, ranchers, or other passersby who happened to be out at night on horseback still claimed to see a white-clad figure on the sagging balcony. A ghost bride, perhaps, or barn owls again. Barn owls, mice, harvestmen spiders, tiny lizards, and crickets were the only remaining residents in the forlorn hotel.

June of 1921 brought flood waters to Glendale when a reservoir dam broke on upper Beaver Creek. Some stables, corrals, and log buildings were torn apart by the water, but the sturdy stone hotel on the hill was left undamaged, only to be ravaged later by fire. The timber, porches, balcony, and roof were destroyed in that blaze, leaving only a stone shell that was once the glory of Glendale.

Cattle now roam through the cottonwoods along Beaver Creek, foraging among tamarix, black-eyed susans, thistle, and a red tangle here and there of autumn Virginia creeper. Spiny clumps of plains prickly pear, with their abundant crimson fruit, and a few stout tree chollas have claimed the ground where the front lawn had been. The black locust tree by the well is barely living; it stands alone. In the chimneys, sparrows have stuffed their nests, and a cool wind blows in the emptiness of Glendale House, softly singing a bittersweet song through the sightless windows and gaping cracks. A lone red-tailed hawk glides above in a cloudless sky. A few meadowlarks sing in the trees while swallows soar over the timeless bluffs.

As the sun's light weaves the grass with long shadows, a cicada high in a golden cottonwood strikes his plaintive note, and the cool breath of twilight descends over Glendale. The cicada falls silent. The screech owl is still. Even crickets fall silent as a sweet voice calls in the silver-blue hour before stars appear. In the girl's voice is an infinite longing as the night breeze catches her words.

"Julian, come back!"

CHAPTER XVI

Phantoms of the Rails

ailroad men had a remarkable talent for collecting excess baggage as they traveled the miles of lonely track. Like mining men, they had their own set of supernatural creatures to keep them company, things from ordinary spooks to lantern-swinging bogeys who directed them down the wrong line. Every engineer had his hoard of favorites stuffed in the engine tender and tried to out-talk every other engineer when it came to exchanging tales of the wraiths.

Among these was a particularly enticing phantom shared by several of the engineers and crewmen on the Atchison, Topeka & Santa Fe Railroad. Tales of the ghost were told and retold in the late 1880s, and many an unfortunate engineer got his ears pulled if he happened to relate the story within earshot of his wife.

The ghost of the AT&SF was that of a beautiful woman with red-gold hair and more curves than the Ophir Loop. She had eyes as blue as the summer sky and a smile that could cause cardiac arrest in the sturdiest of engineers. No one knew who she was or where she came from or how she came to be a ghost, but this was never their concern. They only hoped she wouldn't fade before they could feast their lusting eyes on her.

It was said that she appeared on the AT&SF road between Timpas and Thatcher, never anywhere else. She would be standing along the tracks smiling like a she-devil, or more often she would hop the train, materializing on the platform of a passenger coach or the caboose or sometimes in the engine cab, where the air would be sweetened with the scent of roses. Curiously, no passengers ever saw her. She seemed to reserve herself for the railroad crew only, beckoning, beguiling, and vanishing after they were "hotter'n a steam-piston." One engineer, who was safely unmarried, informed his jealous comrades that the ghost gave him a kiss before departing at Thatcher, a kiss that caused general euphoria and the cessation of all his normal respiratory and circulatory functions. He forgot to stop at the next station, and he never did quite recover.

Men on other lines weren't as blessed as the AT&SF regarding spooks.

The ghost of a little girl repeatedly frayed the nerves of a Rio Grande Southern engineer when she teasingly appeared in the middle of the track and vanished in echoing giggles moments before he would have struck her. Other railroad men were driven to madness by unknown goblins who toyed with the switches, especially at Leadville and Boulder, and who swung misleading signal lanterns that caused all sorts of havoc.

Unlike miners, who were never haunted by the ghosts of deceased hoisting engines or shaft pumps, railroad men were sometimes visited by phantom locomotives and even entire trains. Where a mass of metal derives its "spirit" is beyond the imagination of learned psychics, yet many an expired engine reappeared on the tracks, and many an engine that never existed also popped up to pass the time of day. One story of such an engine was told by Nelson Edwards, an engineer on the Denver & Rio Grande line over Marshall Pass in the early 1880s.

For several months Edwards had been pulling passengers over the pass without interference from the corporeal or spiritual world, but one night as he approached the divide, he imagined the night to be blacker and the air to be sharper and the silence to be more foreboding than usual. An earlier report of a defective rail and hazardous bridge only fueled the engineer's unnamed anxiety.

Leaving the first line of snowsheds, Edwards heard a whistle echoing somewhere among the ice and rocks. At the same time, the signal sounded in his cab to apply the brakes. He pulled the train to a stop, but the conductor yelled at him.

"What did you stop for?" asked the conductor, a bit annoyed. "Get her moving. We've got to pass Nineteen at the switches, and we won't make it unless you pull her open and light out of here."

Edwards threw the lever, sanded the track, and got the train under way again. He heard the strange whistle behind growing louder, sounding danger signals. As he turned a curve, the engineer looked out the cab window. A wild train was climbing fast behind him at a rate certain to end in collision. He pulled the throttle wide open, and the cars lurched through a snow drift and on through the next shed, where the defective rail had been reported. He had to chance the rail; a greater danger threatened behind. He yelled to the conductor to warn the passengers who, upon hearing word of the approaching train, anxiously watched out the windows, believing the rear train was driven by a madman.

When the summit of Marshall Pass was cleared, Edwards shut off steam and allowed gravity to drive the train down the west slope. At another curve he looked back at the pursuing engine, noticing a tall man standing on top of the cars and gesturing frantically. The other train was only 200 yards behind. Edwards could see the engineer leaning out the window with a vicious grin. The stranger's face was broad and flat with a bizarre expression.

The trains were flying close as Edwards approached the dangerous bridge. The engineer thundered across it without any trouble, but the other train was closing in. Coming to the switch, Nineteen was nowhere in sight, and Edwards shot by, but suddenly a red light appeared ahead swinging on the track.

"With that wild train at my rear and some unknown danger ahead," said Edwards, "I was in a hell of a dread. As I put on the brakes I heard the other train's whistle and then no sound at all."

He shot a glance back. At that moment the pursuing train seemed to run against his rear, yet at the same time it toppled from the track down the bank and vanished into the canyon.

"It made me sick," related the engineer. "I heard no cry of injured men or no sound of steam, just the wind in the rocks. The red lantern disappeared too."

Edwards pulled into town ahead of schedule, having no more interference along the road. A weird message was scrawled in the frost on his cab window: "A freight train was recked as yu saw. Not that yu will never make another run. The engine was not under control and four sexshun men wor killed. If yu ever run on this road again yu will be recked."

Being both sensible and superstitious, and apprehensive of misspelled messages, Nelson Edwards resigned the Denver & Rio Grande that morning and took employment with the Union Pacific. The wrecked train he reported was never discovered, not as much as an air-cylinder gasket from it, and word got around that the train was a phantom...or Engineer Edwards was suffering from high altitude. The phantom train never again appeared on Marshall Pass.

Phantoms or the ghosts of wrecked trains did turn up on other tracks, some silent, some whistling, some seen merely as an approaching headlamp with the rest of the locomotive invisible, but no other engineers reported being chased by these. They usually posed no threat, only momentary acrobatics in the region of the heart. On the other hand, there were a few engines in use said to be deadlier than any phantom locomotive, which engineers believed were cursed or possessed by unknown demons.

On the Denver & Rio Grande line between Grand Junction and

Gunnison ran Engine 107, claimed to be the deadliest locomotive on the track. Engineers called her the "Dread 107," or other fitting pet names, and hoped they would never have to take her out. The engine gradually acquired her nasty reputation by escorting a few dozen mortals to their graves. Engineers said "Death sat at her throttle," despite the unmistakable circumstances that acutally were the cause of the various wrecks.

The first disaster occurred when the engine was new. Engineer Bill Duncan drove the train over a bridge where there was none; the river had washed it out. Of course 107 was to blame. The engineer, crew members, and many passengers died. Dead men couldn't be revived, but locomotives could, and the railroad put Dread 107 back on the track with a new crew. Before long Engineer Godfrey met destruction when the train struck a huge boulder. Again many passengers exited for the spirit kingdom, but Dread 107 avoided the scrap heap. She was returned to service and only three months later buried herself in a snowslide in the Black Canyon of the Gunnison with Engineer Bratt at the throttle, killing her quota of mortals for the month. Finally, the D&RG decided to scrap Engine 107 in 1909, but this only released her dreadful ghost, which went a-haunting the old rails. The whistle was heard on foreboding nights near Crystal Creek and the Gunnison River.

Long after the thousands of miles of track in Colorado were abandoned, the longing-for-the-old-days phantom trains hovered near the places they loved. The locomotives, accompanied at times by ghost engineers who were equally attached to the vanished glory of the rails, made haunting runs as if the tracks were still in place. Their echoing whistles have been heard on Corona Pass, Marshall Pass, Hagerman Pass, in South Park, near Salt Springs, and near Ophir, lonesome, distant, and timeless.

The great day of the rail is gone. Only the memories of those days remain, gathered in railroad museums where old locomotives and passenger coaches stand in crowded yards on tracks that lead to nowhere, like the beloved lying in state.

Their paint is peeling. Their windows are dulled or cracked. Their iron is rusted. Their passenger seats collect dust and cobwebs. But talk of them to an old railroad man; the sparkle in his eye says he sees the driver wheels spinning and the cinders flying again. And the glory is back.

CHAPTER XVII

Lanterns On Cemetery Hill

"Love not! Love not! Ye hapless sons of clay!" sang the besotted miners, actually engaging in a good bit more yowling and laughing than singing as the buckboard bumped up the dark road toward Silver Cliff. "Love not! Love not! The thing you love may change."

The fermented flock was returning home from Rosita, where they had celebrated the final hours of celibacy for a friend who was prepared to plunge into wedded bliss...when and if he recovered from bacchic bliss. With gay deviltry, the miners wailed out the words of the popular John Blockley tune until they came in sight of the Silver Cliff Cemetery. One of the men raised a bottle to the beloved dead. Another raised a bottle to the devil. J.W. Arette, driving the two-mule wagon, began singing, "I'll plant a rose upon thy grave, to bloom the sunny summer through—" The others joined in the song like choleric jackasses braying for a dose of calomel.

"A ghost!" cried Arette, abruptly halting the mules. "By my aunt's mustache, it's a ghost!"

The buckboard had stopped at the cemetery gate. The miners, those who could still see, stared at the silent tombstones and crosses. A small, bright blue flame flickered on the edge of a granite stone.

"A ghost!" whispered Arette as he cautiously looped the reins around the seat brace. He climbed down. "Shall we introduce ourselves, friends?"

That starry May night in 1882, six jolly topers shambled into the Silver Cliff Cemetery, resolved to make the acquaintance of a blue ghost. As they approached the eerie light in a brave knot, the flame appeared to leap away. It flickered from the top of another tombstone, but as the men drew near, the light again sprang away. Soon six jolly topers were tripping over themselves trying to catch the teasing ghost and other blue lights that had joined the sport. Each time a man came within catching distance of a ghost light, the light would disappear, only to reappear on another stone. One of the party, J.J. Hutchinson, screamed that a ghost had gotten him. He fell down on a grave and there remained to illustrate vividly the term "dead drunk," until Arette and G.C. Ballard escorted his remains to the buck-board. At that point the men decided to complete the last half mile of their journey into town.

In Silver Cliff J.W. Arette informed others of the strange lights in the cemetery. Observing J.W.'s state of progressed intoxication, the men merely humored him, asking him if he saw the ghost of this or that deceased citizen. Ballard cut in, assuring the cynics that there were no actual ghosts or spirits, but that there were definitely strange lights in the cemetery.

"The six of you were well lit, to be sure," said C.E. Hunter. "And certainly strange."

Both Arette and Ballard insisted they saw the lights. They contin-ued to insist over the next several days, trying to convince some of the men to take a midnight jaunt to the cemetery to see for them-selves. Finally, a small wager aided toward that purpose.

At the end of the week a crew including Arette, Ballard, Hutchinson, C.E. Hunter, Josiah Caine, and T.A. Powell walked to the cemetery, which had been established in 1878, for the grand encounter. Properly fortified against the chill spring night with a fair amount of warming whiskey, the men sang loudly down the road. When they reached the hilltop site, Hutchinson lost courage, vaguely recalling a sneak attack by a spook in the place. He was expressing an urgent desire to return to town when suddenly he caught sight of a faint light on the top of a marble gravestone.

"They're here," he whispered. "They've seen us."

The others turned to see the flickering light. Fascinated, Hunter watched it move across the edge of the stone and disappear. He turned excitedly to Hutchinson, clapping him on the shoulders. There was some speculating as to what actually caused the light; Hutchinson quickly said it was the eyes of a ghost or a ghost's lantern, hoping he might return to town before the "attack." Josiah Caine suggested the light was St. Elmo's fire, an electrical phenomenon he had seen on mules' ears before a storm. Hunter agreed. He had heard of this oc-curring on ships' masts and other pointed objects.

As the man walked around the cemetery and observed the blue lights leap from tombstone to tombstone, they noticed that the odd behavior of the lights seemed to be contrary to the initial theory. Of course the men continued to fortify themselves against the chill air, so naturally the lights behaved bizarrely. There was more talk of ghosts and ghost lanterns. By the time they returned to Silver Cliff, they were convinced the lights belonged to the spirit world, especially

Hutchinson, who was certain he saw several, probably a dozen or
more, of those spirits carrying lanterns as they flitted among the
graves.

A few weeks later C.E. Hunter led an expedition to the cemetery
with the notion of studying the ghost lights in the darkness of night.
This was strictly a scientific investigation. Among the distinguished
company were William M. Burckes, an assayer; James J. Rowen, an attorney;
a photographer; two ladies in the millinery business; a saloon keeper;
and J.W. Arette, an ordinary miner.

Mrs. Wells and Mrs J.A. Doyle, the milliners, tramped from tombstone
to tombstone, ritualistically calling off the names of the deceased
while the rest of the company stood about, hands in pockets, waiting
for the lights. As the stars slowly turned in the heavens, the group
walked up and down, north and south over the cemetery grounds.
After another hour of north and south, with a dash east and west
for variety, the investigators began to murmur against Hunter. No
lights, no ghosts, no bats, no anything but an addlepated rabbit
presented itself.

"Where are the lights, Mr. Hunter?" said James Rowen as if he were
cross-examining a criminal witness. "If I were the suspicious sort, I'd
think you lured us out to this place under cover of darkness for
sinister purposes, Mr. Hunter. Of course I am not suspicious. But
where are the lights?"

Hunter and Arette defended the lights; perhaps they were on holi-
day, or something.

"Or something, sir?" said Mrs. Wells, poking him with a long finger.
"I think it is a hoax. And not a very good one."

Mrs. Wells and Mrs. Doyle set off for Silver Cliff. Shortly the attorney, assayer, and saloon keeper followed. Disappointed and angry with
the lights, Hunter sulked at the cemetery gate. He couldn't understand
where the blue flames had gone; he had seen them on his own several times since his introduction to them. He began to suspect again
that the lights were something other than an electrical phenomenon.

Just as he turned to go he saw a bright flicker on a nearby
tombstone.

"The lights!" he shouted to the retreating skeptics. "Come back!"

John A. Wilmers, the saloon keeper, and James Rowen returned
quickly to the cemetery. William M. Burckes ran up beside them,
stopping enthralled as he saw a blue light leap heavenward. As the
men moved toward another light on a tombstone, a blue flame sprang
from the side of Burckes's head.

"Burckes!" gasped Hunter. "Did you feel that?"

The light had gone unnoticed by the assayer, but for the remaining time in the cemetery Burckes held his hand delicately to his ear as if he were keeping a moth trapped there.

Attempting to examine the eerie lights, the men could never really get close to one, whether they rushed on the light or crept slowly toward it. Rowen all but broke his chin when he made an overly enthusiastic dash toward a flicker and struck his jaw on the edge of a tombstone. After that he proposed they adjourn for the night.

Back in town the lights were discussed and rediscussed. There were as many opinions as to what caused the lights as there were witnesses to them. A surprising number of gentlemen favored ghosts. Others argued for St. Elmo's fire. Some advocated will-o'-the-wisps, a phosphorescent light said to be caused by spontaneous combustion of gases emitted by rotting organic matter, usually occurring in swamps or marshes. Perhaps the lights were caused by certain minerals in the burial grounds, or unknown gas, or some sort of reflection. Or ghosts again...Definitely ghosts, added J.W. Arette. No one could prove any theory. The lights' behavior fit no specific pattern, and the weird blue flames were soon referred to as "ghost lights" by the residents of Wet Mountain Valley.

Many a fellow used the ghost lights as an excuse to get his sweetheart to the hill at night. Many a prankster used the lights as an opportunity to scare the wig off a scientific researcher or spiritualist. Two young ladies, the daughters of a justice of the peace, spent several summer nights in 1889 pretending to be the ghosts behind the lights. Dressed in black, the girls slipped around the cemetery behind bushes and tombstones, carrying small lanterns with blue-tinted globes. In this manner they frightened several citizens, until one man caught on to their game. Dressed as a cadaver and waiting peacefully in an open grave, he sprang on the girls, ending their ghostly career. After that they were said to have given up pranks of even the simplest sort.

As years passed the mysterious ghost lights were sought out by residents, tourists, spiritualists, and a few science-oriented individuals. People had grown accustomed to the phenomenon, and everyone sported his own theory. Generally, the Silver Cliff Cemetery was said to be haunted. Although the lights weren't visible all the time, they could be seen most often on overcast nights, appearing to dance among the graves.

A Denver scientist named Charles H. Howe tried to discover the cause of the phenomenon in 1895. With a photographer, Joseph Collier, and an electrical engineer, John Crawford, Howe studied the lights for a week in May. On only two of the seven nights did the men actually see the blue flickers, but they became convinced that the lights were St. Elmo's fire when for several minutes they appeared to dance on top of Collier's camera tripod. Both nights when the lights were seen, the sky was reported to be overcast.

Whenever mediums or spiritualists got into the act, they proclaimed the lights to be held by ghosts. One man from Pueblo, Arthur Knotts, said the lights were actually the ghosts themselves, seen only as a dim blue flickering by human eyes, but seen as the forms of men and women when viewed through special smoked glass. Quite possibly Knotts was willing to provide, for a nominal fee, the necessary smoked glass.

Decade after decade Silver Cliff Cemetery enticed a trickle of curiosity seekers to its gate. Hundreds of people saw the blue lights. Some years the lights vanished altogether. Other years there was less interest in them. In 1949, 1956, and 1963 the ghost lights again attracted widespread attention, being especially active in April in 1956 when snow blanketed Wet Mountain Valley. The lights were yet unexplained. The popular theory at the time was that they were swamp angels, will-o'-the-wisps, or similar phenomena found in marshy places and caused by decaying matter. Ray De Wall, then publisher of the *Wet Mountain Tribune* in nearby Westcliffe, disagreed, for the cemetery was on a dry hill. Yucca and cacti grew on the graves.

The blue lights, faithfully disappearing as approached, still flickered on tombstones, between fences, and uncommonly on a head or two. They were seen best and brightest on polished granite tombstones. Oddly, at Ula Cemetery, a few miles north and nearer to water, the lights never occurred.

Joe Payton, publisher of the *Wet Mountain Tribune* in 1963, suggested the lights were caused by reflections from electrical lights throughout the valley. But one night when the lights were off in Silver Cliff and Westcliffe, the cemetery's little blue ghosts still flickered.

Since the ghost lights were first seen, Silver Cliff has become nearly a ghost herself. Her riproaring, loud, and boisterous days are long passed, her thousands of citizens long gone. She has lost the coveted county seat to Westcliffe and lost the once enormous revenues from her silver mines. More citizens sleep in her cemetery than live in her wistful, far-flung, but destitute city boundaries. Yet she has not lost her pride or her ghosts.

Many a ghost has chosen to visit Silver Cliff's abandoned, listing houses, but they can come or go. It is the cemetery ghosts with their blue lanterns who put a spark in the eyes of the town's remaining citizens. The blue lights have baffled generations and are still sought by valley residents and tourists. Countless people have stories about them to recite and theories to share. Yet the lights remain a mystery.

At 8011 feet, Silver Cliff Cemetery overlooks the broad, serene Wet Mountain Valley, facing the velvet-shouldered majesty of the Sangre de Cristo Range. A small sign standing at the cemetery gate briefly tells of the uncanny blue lights. Yucca, grass, bushes, and wildflowers crowd the memorials to past citizens in this quiet, deserted place swept by centuries of wind. Even in sunlight there is a sense of mystery and wonder hovering around the cracked, leaning stones, a sense sharpened by the sudden silence of buzzing grasshoppers and chittering sparrows, leaving only the sound of a sighing breeze across the hill.

When the sun sets and purple shadows shroud the valley, the mystery creeps to life like ghosts coming out of their graves. There is silence and anticipation. One can almost feel a presence in the deep shadows, a presence without substance, an image without shape.

Then from the point of a granite tombstone flares a small, shimmering light of blue. It taunts . . . and vanishes into the mysterious night.

CHAPTER XVIII

An Unexpected Passenger

"here's a bloomin' fool on the track!" cried the engineer to the fireman, both cursing and praying the train could be stopped in time. "Good Lord—we've hit him!"

Instantly there was a sickening thud as the cowcatcher slammed into the man, hurling his body upward, where it spun off the nose below the lamp and was slung into the darkness. When the train came to a shrieking, jerking halt, alarmed passengers rushed to the windows, stretching their necks, peering into the night to see what had happened. Anxious questions and disturbed chatter filled the coaches. A little girl awoke on her mother's lap and began to cry. An old woman muttered that they were all doomed. Coming from another car, a shaggy professor brought word: the train had struck a man.

The engineer, fireman, passenger conductor, and other crew members, along with a porter and several passengers, bolted from the sighing train, some with a vague hope the victim was still alive, others with an unabashed morbid curiosity to see him dead.

A small trace of blood and tissue clung to the front of the locomotive, but the man's body was nowhere to be found. Searching through the trackside weeds with lanterns held aloft, the engineer and others finally came upon the mutilated remains of a deer. The unsuspecting creature was freshly dead and appeared to have met that end swiftly in the path of a train. Questions were put to the engineer: had the animal's form, indistinctly seen, been altered by his fancy and the darkness of night into that of a human? The engineer would have been greatly relieved to have that be the case, but he was certain he had seen a man—a man in a dark suit of clothes, not a tan deer. It was argued that the event was instantaneous: how certain could he be that he perceived a man? The carcass of a deer and the absence of any human corpse indicated otherwise, and the fireman couldn't say what he saw. Shaking his head, the engineer confessed his confusion. He proposed that the deer was struck by an earlier train, and the body they were looking for lay somewhere nearby.

"We can't search all night," said one man, as D.A. Graham, the passenger conductor, interrupted the discussion.

Graham handed over to the engineer a new black derby with a gray silk band and a single red feather adorning it. He explained he had found the hat on the opposite side of the track a few yards south of Dry Creek (Van Bibber Creek) where the engineer had first seen the man. .or thought such.

"Deer don't wear hats," mumbled the engineer.

Conceding that deer were usually unfamiliar with haberdasheries, the fireman suggested the derby was possibly lost in a windstorm and there for days; after all, the wagon road was on that side of the tracks. If there was a body, they could find it in the morning, but there were serious doubts that any corpse would be located. Sighing, feeling at a loss, the engineer boarded the train and took it the remaining few miles into Golden.

The Jefferson County coroner, Dr. Joseph Anderson, was informed that a man had possibly been struck by the Colorado Central locomotive 20 July 1881, immediately south of Van Bibber Creek on the Ralston Station to Golden track. He was told that a search had been made, but that only the remains of a deer were found. The derby was turned over to the coroner.

Unsatisfied with mere possibilities, Dr. Anderson, accompanied by George Albert, William B. Wentworth, and Constable J.A. Baker, drove out the following morning to the scene of the accident. They found what was left of the deer on the east side of the track and upon examining the remains, concluded that the animal had definitely collided with a locomotive. Yet for his own satisfaction, Dr. Anderson continued the search for the mysterious missing man.

Toward noon, the men were considering abandoning the effort when Wentworth discovered in the track bed a fragment of linen collar with a ruby button set still attached. This only added more fog to the situation. Was the fragment recent? Was it the victim's? Where the devil was the body? Could a man be so utterly dismembered by a train as not to be found? Dr. Anderson doubted the possibility. After much consideration he decided there was no case, and that all the evening train had struck was the deer.

Later that day, a coal miner, who had heard the story, arrived at the sheriff's office. He informed Sheriff J.M. Johnson, Jr. that he had been on the road the previous night, close to morning, when he saw a wagon and a couple of men with lanterns. They were beside the C.C. track near Van Bibber Creek when he watched them load something into the wagon. They extinguished the lanterns and, turning the wagon around, drove south toward Golden.

Fond of mysteries as long as they could be solved, Sheriff Johnson took a trot around his room, mentally viewing each angle and corner of this new intelligence. He inquired if the miner could discern what the men carried. No, the miner was too far away at the time. Was it possible, considering size and shape, that their burden was a man? Yes, possible, but the miner wouldn't swear to it. He added that the men carried it between them, placing it carefully in the wagon. Sheriff Johnson, not wanting to be perplexed all alone, related this information to the coroner.

For days Dr. Anderson was distracted by the mystery and hounded by doubts and questions. Was a man murdered on the track and then his body removed secretly? But what sense was there in that—he could have been left for a suicide. Was he a suicide whose remains were conveyed away by shamed friends or relatives? Or was there any man at all? The men the coal miner saw could have been poachers or rustlers or God-knows-whats. There was the engineer's statement of seeing a man, there was the derby, the collar fragment, a dead deer, and a coal miner's tale. Was it all related? What did it all add up to? Was he trying to infer too much from unconnected circumstances and scarce evidence? A corpse would definitely improve matters.

Finally, as the proper corpse refused to make its way to the coroner's offices, and as Dr. Anderson had many more important matters at hand, especially his private practice as a physician, the mystery of the derbyless gentleman was tossed out with the chicken bones. The locomotive engineer and D.A. Graham were perhaps the only persons who believed there was a man killed by the 20 July train. No one else appeared to lose sleep over the unknown, unnamed victim. Until he came back.

Less than a month later, as a Colorado Central train crossed Van Bibber Creek, an unearthly groan rose up from beneath the engine. Inside one of the passenger coaches a shadowy figure formed in the seat across the aisle from a Boulder woman named Mrs. Walling. Upon seeing the newly arrived passenger from the corner of her eye, Mrs. Walling quickly turned toward him, only to be reproached by an empty seat. She shrugged, and in so doing again noticed, at a sidelong glance, the elusive stranger. Fearing to turn toward the vision, she contemplated it from a shrewd angle, taking note that it was a man with a disturbing countenance and peculiar manner. The shadowy man's eye caught Mrs. Walling's; she screamed and fainted dead away.

Several passengers, along with the conductor, D.A. Graham, rushed to assist the unconscious Mrs. Walling. She was propped in her seat, fanned, pinched, and assaulted with spirits of ammonia until her wits were restored. Immediately she told the hovering Samaritans she had seen a ghost. The ghost, she explained, was a bearded man wearing a black coat and waistcoat and a black derby with a gray ribbon. A cold draft emanated from him. "An evil, cold draft," Mrs. Walling thoughtfully added. But the most distressing, the most repugnant thing was that this ghost looked at her. He looked right *into* her. His expression caused her to swoon.

If those in attendance upon Mrs. Walling had any opinions about the ghost or about the woman's state of mind, they kept them secret, trying to keep her quiet and relaxed. Seeing in their faces that few believed her, Mrs. Walling grew all the louder, insisting that what she saw she indeed saw and no one was to say otherwise. Eventually Graham assured her he believed every word she uttered, and he shivered at the conclusion.

In the following months other passengers encountered the man in the derby. He appeared at the time the trains crossed Van Bibber Creek enroute to Golden, never materializing when the trains went the opposite direction. One man, a boardinghouse proprietor from Denver named Peter Dornin, had the translucent passenger appear in the seat beside him. Dornin later described the apparition as exceedingly unpleasant, negative, and exuding a turbulence or vehemence he was unable to fully explain. Also, the ghost had a foul scent about him, "not unlike moldy vegetation." Lasting only a few seconds, the vision left Dornin extremely uncomfortable, angry, and nauseated.

With each appearance on passing trains, the bearded phantom grew more vicious. His physical abilities were little thwarted by his gaseous state. He was said to have burst the glass globes of the lamps in a restaurant car, causing great distress and panic among the diners. He was accused of removing the hair stuffings of passenger seats and breaking the fire door on a coach heating stove. One time he stamped vigorously on a coach roof and groaned and moaned until a number of gentlemen passengers went out on the platform to ascertain the cause of the disturbance. When they saw him, he immediately vaporized. In another incident, he raised and lowered the window blinds until the slats broke. One passenger, Mrs. Lettie Eichter, reported to the conductor that an obnoxious man presumed to abruptly occupy the empty seat beside her and to blow foul cigar smoke directly into her face. She described the stranger as a large, bearded man wearing a derby. The conductor found no trace of this passenger where Mrs. Eichter said he had been. Many times this volatile gentleman was blamed for the terrible odors found lingering in the mail coach, or the brakes suddenly jamming, or any other thing that went wrong.

Certainly the ghost couldn't be expected to limit himself to trains. He appeared a few times on inspection handcars and was seen merely standing in the track by passersby on horseback. In 1894 the foul phantom threw himself on an unsuspecting chicken farmer, materializing in the farmer's wagon. In an instant the attacker swept all the chicken crates—chickens included—out of the wagon and without farewell or explanation departed into the air.

Some revelers on the road near Van Bibber Creek in 1897 were driving along in their two-horse trap late at night when their horses stopped short. The animals, no matter how coaxed or threatened, refused to move. Out of the stillness of the night a groaning sound rose, soon accompanied by an ominous figure standing in the track, looking at the revelers. The phantom, in gentleman's attire and a derby, hissed at them. He showed his teeth in a ghastly grimace, as if he was considering sinking those incisors into the young men. He flew at them, and a deadly conflict ensued. One of the revelers, Jeremy Peets, claimed the ghost did bite him and afterward had scars to prove it. The brief combat was described by Peets as a horrible experience. He felt as if a flock of crazed and rotted pigeons had descended upon him and his companions with a violent appetite. The ghost was said to have claimed the territory near the place of his demise, and he had no kindness for those he regarded as trespassers.

Over the years the mysterious ghost was the subject of fireside discussion and Halloween tales. Many people spread word that he was the spirit of a man who had killed himself on the track because of an unrequited love. A few people insisted he was a devil or evil goblin. As with most haunted places, youngsters ventured to the spot on dares to see if the ghost would oblige them and scare them to death.

The railroad track north of Golden was eventually abandoned and removed, and a modern paved road (Highway 93) was put in its place, but the phantom remained in his territory. After 1920 he was rarely mentioned, but a few persons in recent years claimed to have seen him or felt his presence, including a prominent Golden businessman.

The ghost has dwindled to no more than an inky, evil negative force or power, sometimes seen near Van Bibber Creek as a dust devil or small cloud. He is still disagreeably cold, damp, foul, and unpleasant, occupying himself as an unwanted hitchhiker, not bothering to wait for a car to stop. Without proper introduction he usurps the passenger seat next to a lone motorist traveling south on Highway 93 after dark. His features are no longer distinguishable, but he is recognized as man or the empty husk of someone's baser personality. He seems to steal the air and impair the reflexes. Violent emotions escape from the foggy form as he attempts to speak, delivering only groans. In his desperation and anger he tries to reach the motorist, but his hands are no longer functioning as individual appendages.

With a terrible groan he tries again to reach the motorist, the faint shape of fingers clawing out of the dark vapor, clawing, twisting... reaching...and he fades into nothingness as the car speeds into Golden.

CHAPTER XIX

To Kill A Barber

 "lood! Blood!" screamed the mulatto girl in terror. "It's full of blood! Get it out of here! Get it away! Oh God! Blood all over my hands!"

Rushing into the room, Belle Worden found the girl sobbing hysterically on the floor.

"Mattie, you must stop," ordered Belle, shaking her. "Stop, Mattie."

"It's full of blood," cried Mattie. "The ewer is full of blood!"

Belle looked into the ewer where it rested innocently in its basin by Mattie's bed.

"There's only water in it," returned Belle. "Nothing more."

"No! No! I saw it!" screamed Mattie.

Belle slapped her. "You must stop! Someone will surely hear you." She pulled the girl to her ample bosom, stroking Mattie's hair until she was at last calmed.

Mattie Lemon was one of six girls who worked in Belle Worden's house at 578 Holladay Street, a rather moldy establishment catering to the needs of Denver's lustful gentlemen. Since March of 1884, Mattie had occasionally fallen victim to horrible nightmares or hallucinations during which she swore the ewer was filled with blood or her hands were stained with it or her bedroom walls were spattered with it. Belle usually managed to calm her, give her something to induce deep sleep, and put her to bed.

Belle was anxious about Mattie's state of mind. She knew the reason for the girl's terror but could only hope Mattie did not give in to it, thereby bringing ruin upon the house. Some clients were already spreading rumors that the house was haunted, and this did little to encourage business. Belle told her fears to her lover, Charles Smith, a hack driver who brought many customers to the Worden brothel.

Unfortunately, Charley could offer no solace. Instead he told Belle he was certain he was being haunted in connection with the same thing torturing Mattie. He related to her how night after night, when he was driving the hack through the streets alone, he heard a ghastly, gasping whisper repeating, "Stop...stop...stop..." Then there would be rapping on the front glass. Charley thought surely he was going mad, for each time he would stop, quickly open the door of the cab, and no one, absolutely no one, was inside. Belle urged him to pay it no heed; surely it was only a malignant imagination.

That night Charley was taking a fare to Belle's place when he heard the slow, gasping words, "Stop...stop...stop." He stopped, angered that his passenger would annoy him deliberately. Pulling open the door, he saw that the gentleman in the seat had a look of terror on his face, his eyes fixed on the corner opposite.

"My God!" choked the man, "My God!" His hands, shaking violently, went to his mouth. "My God!" The man fled past Charley and on down the street.

From the dark corner within the hack, a Negro man looked hard at Charley, slowly grinning. The Negro was clearly dead, his face a blue-gray, his eyes flat and sunken, his nose and cheeks decomposed, and fresh blood on his forehead. Charley's nostrils were filled with the nauseating stench of rotting flesh.

Slamming the cab door, Charley cursed at the thing inside, shouting for it to go away. He beat on the window and kicked at the door.

"Stop...stop...stop..." came the ghastly voice.

Charley covered his ears with his hands. In a frenzy, he kicked the coach again and again.

"What's the matter, Mr. Smith?" called the rheumatic Mrs. Archer from her door. "Have you lost your fare again, Mr. Smith?"

Charley glowered at her, and she gave him a knowing nod. She closed her door.

At Belle's, Charley demanded whiskey to incapacitate the snakes that seemed to be twisting in his stomach. After much drinking, he told Belle of his encounter with the dead man who wasn't quite dead.

"Only a few doors from here," said Charley, "my fare went down the street like—" He laughed sardonically.

Berry Gates, the Negro boyfriend of Mattie Lemon, scoffed at the tale. He accused Charley of fabricating all of it just to scare them and would have attacked him, had Belle not intervened. He warned Charley that he had best keep his mouth shut. Belle reminded them that they all must keep quiet.

Extremely agitated and feeling sick, Charley Smith returned to his hack. The hour was late. He peered into the dark leather interior to make certain it was unoccupied. Satisfied with this inspection, he extinguished the lamp marked with the number "61" that hung at the left of the door. His hours over, he was determined to go straight to the livery without picking up a single person, even if they had broken legs. He climbed onto the box, gripping the horsewhip, dreading the several dark streets between him and his destination.

As the horse cantered along, its hooves clacking with the rattling coach wheels, Charley glanced into the window at his lower back to make certain he had not acquired any unwanted passengers. Still nothing appeared in the seats. The May night was cold and windy and rain began to fall. Pulling his coat collar around his ears, Charley whipped the horse into a gallop. Something thunked the bottom of the hack. Charley nearly flew from his perch on the box.

"Just a rock, just a rock," he told himself, but his heart was pounding hard.

He glanced around to make another check on his vehicle.

"No!" he gasped as his eyes fell on the glowing lamp with 61 painted on it. Inside, the lamp illuminated the ghastly face of the dead Negro, smiling slightly as he nodded to Charley.

"No! No!" cried Charley, thrashing his horse.

"Stop...stop...stop..." said the passenger. "Stop..."

Charley, racing dangerously fast, passed the livery and went careening down the next street. Finally he got himself and the horse under control and delivered the hack at the livery. He was reprimanded for having sweated the horse, but he heard nothing, thought of nothing save escape.

The next day, 25 May 1884, was a sunny Sunday. Just below the bridge where Holladay Street crossed Cherry Creek, several boys were playing in the creekbed. From the night's rain there had been flooding, leaving the water slightly higher than usual, exposing rocks and something whitish near what the boys had thought was a bag of sand.

One boy running along in the shallow water yelled to his friend, "Hey! What's that? See near our sand bag?"

He and his friends investigated. A younger boy became sick when they realized the object was a decomposed hand, and their "sand bag," on which they had played the last few weeks, was the body belonging to that hand.

Running up the creek like startled hares, the boys breathlessly told other youngsters of their discovery.

"There's a dead body in Cherry Creek!"

Word reached the police via the father of one of the boys.

Coroner Miller, Denver police officers, a detective, the boys, and their parents descended on the corpse like flies on raw meat. The body was examined, discussed, and dug out of the sand to be transported to the coroner's rooms.

In his rooms, Coroner Miller made further examinations. The dead man was clad in a heavy overcoat, vest, trousers, knit underclothes, flannel socks, new shoes, and a white shirt marked "J.H.F." Badly decomposed, with the nose and hair mostly gone, except for a small mustache, the man was tentatively identified as a Negro or mulatto, between thirty and forty years old. He was five feet, six inches tall and of medium build. There was a deep wound above the right eye, which the coroner believed was caused by a blunt instrument.

After removing the clothes from the corpse, Miller found a large hole immediately below the breast bone. He speculated that it might have been caused by a charge of buckshot, yet there was no hole in the clothing.

Dr. Hamer, a police surgeon, performed an autopsy and determined that the dead man was a victim of foul play. He had received a severe blow to the head and the thrust of a large butcher knife to the breast. Dr. Hamer concluded the man was undressed when he received the fatal wounds.

Meanwhile, Coroner Miller had examined the contents of the man's pockets, including keys, coins, and a Union Depot check, number 114. This last item led the coroner to a valise at the Union Station, containing barber tools with the name John H. Fitzgerald carved on the razor handles. In the valise was also a book filled with poetry and barber recipes. On the back cover was an engraved silver medal reading, "God bless our home—Mattie, John—1879."

The murdered man was identified as John H. Fitzgerald, and Denver detectives lost no time in reconstructing his last hours. A business card from Fitzgerald's pocket led them to Green's Little Barbershop, 354 Nineteenth Street.

W.H. Green, owner of the shop, said he knew Fitzgerald.

"He came to Denver March 16," Green said, "to get barber tools. He's from Leadville where he's got a wife. I think her name is Mattie. I remember him having a lot of money with him."

Green had last seen Fitzgerald on 19 March.

The detectives sent for Mrs. Mattie Fitzgerald, who arrived in Denver on the next train. She verified the identification of her husband and described various articles he carried in his pockets, which she later identified, but noted that his hunting case gold watch with a wide bar chain and horseshoe charm was missing.

"I hadn't seen my husband since March 16," she said. "He had about $400 when he left Leadville. I received a telegram from him on

March 18, last, saying that he would return the next day.

"George Lyons of Denver came to Leadville to see me, asking if my husband had returned. This was within a month after John had disappeared. Mr. Lyons came twice. Lyons was no friend of my husband. John had loaned him some money."

Detectives paid George Lyons a visit at his gambling establishment at 388 Holladay Street. There they learned from a man, who refused to identify himself, that Fitzgerald was at Green's Gambling Den the night of 19 March. The anonymous friend said he and Fitzgerald were at a game where the latter lost a few dollars—no more than twenty-five—and had flashed a large roll of bills.

Later, when the two left the gambling house, they were approached by Berry Gates.

"That darky," said the man, "had been in Green's place lurking about and seen the money John had. He told him there was a place just up the street where the girls are sweet for a night. I told him he best forget it; Gates was nothin' but a low life."

The man related that Fitzgerald was feeling good and, since he had a few more hours before his train departed for Leadville, he accepted the invitation. As Fitzgerald went with Gates toward Belle Worden's house, that was the last the friend saw of him.

Questioning Belle's neighbors, the detectives found no one could recall seeing Fitzgerald leave the brothel.

One neighbor, Mrs. Martha Gregory, told them, "I remember being startled by two or three cries of 'murder' which seemed to come from Belle Worden's place. It was about the middle of March. The cries seemed to be smothered. It was between one or two o'clock in the morning. It was very dark and raining, so I didn't see what the matter was."

Mrs. Lizzie Archer, five doors down from the Worden place, was the neighborhood's ears. She eagerly shared her knowledge with the police detectives.

"It was about three months ago," said Mrs. Archer. "I was lying in bed with the rheumatism, don't you know, and nearly asleep. I heard three cries of 'murder.' Don't know exactly what night it was....Well, I told my help to go to the door. She's a good lady, don't you know, takes good care of me. This was between one and two in the morning. It was raining, cold, a bit like rain and snow. Come to think of it, it was on Wednesday night and the middle of March. Nellie Rice always comes on Wednesday, don't you know, and she'd been here that afternoon."

Mrs. Archer added that several people in the neighborhood were certain the Worden house was haunted, as many gentlemen would leave in a terrible hurry as if they had seen a ghost or something.

"Now where do you suppose they would get such a notion," continued Mrs. Archer. "Well, sir, I'll tell you! About half an hour after the cries that Wednesday, I heard men walking rapidly up the street. I remember that hack driver, Mr. Smith. He's an odd one, to be sure. Always losing his fares. The people about Worden's have been acting terribly funny for three months past. We had a fuss and she don't speak to me now, don't you know.

"The next day I walked round the corner and saw blood on the pavement in front of Worden's. She took up carpets and I thought it a mighty funny time to clean house. Imagine! In the middle of March."

On 3 June the police arrested Belle Worden, Mattie Lemon, Berry Gates, and later Charles Smith. That day a gold watch was found on the Worden premises and identified by Mrs. Fitzgerald as her husband's.

The following day the detectives made a thorough search of the house. After fruitless digging in the back yard, they went to the cellar in hopes of finding the murder weapon or other evidence. In the cellar they uncovered a linen sheet, a comforter, and a flannel blanket, all heavily saturated with blood. They had been kept moist by the damp earth.

The four suspects were put in the county jail to await their trial on 6 December. Despite their pleas of innocence, they were held without bond. Charley expressed relief to no longer be driving the hack, and the others entreated him to say nothing more.

Public cab number 61 had a new driver during the summer months named Rudolph Barr. Only a few days after he began driving the hack, he noticed something uncanny about it. A man appeared to be seated inside, but when Barr opened the door, no one was there. He tried to dismiss this as reflections in the glass, until one evening when he was driving along Holladay Street without a fare and his horse bolted. As the coach careened down the street with Barr gripping the reins for dear life, he heard a hideous voice calling on him to stop. Like a hoarse whisper it slowly repeated, "Stop...stop...stop."

The hack finally came to a standstill on the Holladay Street bridge over Cherry Creek. Barr climbed off the box feeling a bit unnerved and pulled open the coach door. The rotting corpse of a Negro man was slung across the seat. Barr slammed the door and was sick in the street. At length he pulled himself together and, believing he should inform the police at once, reopened the door with shaking hands to make certain he had not imagined the scene.

Nothing was in the hack.

It took all of Barr's nerve to return the hack to the livery that night.

On succeeding evenings Barr heard the spectral command for him to stop the hack. When he was alone on deserted streets he urged the horse into a gallop, praying all the while to his favorite saint. Word soon spread that public cab 61 was haunted, and several pale passengers verified hearing the voice while riding with Barr. The hack driver was certain the ghost was John Fitzgerald lost in time and crying out to be spared, though Barr was uncertain as to why Fitzgerald chose to haunt the coach. But the hauntings were not confined to that vehicle.

Passersby and neighbors of the now-empty Worden brothel said they heard stifled cries coming from the house. The last of Belle's girls to abandon the establishment claimed she saw blood spattered darkly over the ewer and basin in Mattie's room, and she heard ghostly whisperings around her. On her final night there she heard a horrible gurgling noise and the sound of something being dragged down the hall. No one cared to remain in the house, and children hurried by it.

Charley Smith heard the tales and read of them in the newspapers. He could no longer bear the threat of the ghost still about town. Perhaps it would come for him. Charley, in fear, gave a complete confession to the police of the murder of John Fitzgerald.

Quite pleased, the police informed the other three that Charley had confessed on behalf of all four to ease his conscience and encourage the others to do the same. When Belle, Mattie, and Berry confronted Charley with this news, Charley exclaimed with an oath he did no such thing. He called the police liars. He cursed the entire justice system, but to no avail.

Continuing to plead innocent, the four went to trial. At its conclusion 26 December 1884, they were found guilty of murder and sentenced by Judge Elliot to ten years hard labor in the state penitentiary at Canon City.

Three years later Mattie Lemon became gravely ill. Although under a doctor's care, she rapidly grew worse. On 20 June 1887 Mattie asked for a priest.

A priest was not available, so a Protestant minister was obtained. In her cell Mattie related the details of the murder.

"Early in the morning," said Mattie, "Fitzgerald was sleeping in my room, undressed, and as we all knew he had money, it was suggested that Berry Gates first kill him, then rob him. Belle Worden wasn't there."

She described to the minister and doctor how Berry had stabbed Fitzgerald as he lay in bed, and how the blood spurted on the walls and floor, making Mattie sick. Berry, believing the wound was not a fatal one, took the large ewer and crashed it with a terrible blow into the dying man's forehead.

"Then we sent for Charley Smith," continued Mattie, "and the two men dressed the dead man and put him in Smith's hack to take him away. Belle was very much excited when she heard the man was killed and said that we must all keep our mouths shut."

Since dawn was breaking, Mattie told them, Charley hid the body in an abandoned shack. Then that night he and Berry buried the body in Cherry Creek, though none too thoroughly.

Mattie was left alone in her cell for a few moments while the doctor conferred with the minister and the warden. Upon his return, the doctor found Mattie dead. Her confession lightened the sentence for Belle Worden and Charley Smith, but they received the news of her death with heavy hearts.

When at last he was released, Charley returned to Denver. But the old familiar places, Holladay Street, the accusing eye of Mrs. Archer, the vacant windows of passing hacks, reminded him of that fateful night of 19 March 1884. He could not reckon with the thought that he might hear the whisperings again, or turn around and see the dead Fitzgerald staring at him. He would never forget that face...never.

Charley Smith left the state.

CHAPTER XX

Columbines From A Far Place

n a hilltop cemetery overlooking Central City, a solemn shaft of marble points heavenward, sacred to the memory of the Cameron family. Tinted by passing years and copper lichens, the monument bears the names of a father, a mother, and an only child, their son John Edward. Steller's jays and warblers sing mourning songs on this hill among the listing stones and long forgotten secrets. There is solitude here, and wonder, and mystery.

When the aspen have yet to push forth their leaves in April, and the tangle of wild grass is only a green blush in the Masonic Cemetery, a wild yellow rose blooms beside the Cameron monument. Sprung from dry ground, the rose leans gently toward the marble headstone as if in tenderness for those buried beneath. No other flowers bloom in meadow or on mountain. Snow still hides in the deep shadows, and yet, woven into the branches of the rose are woodland ferns and a spray of resplendent blue columbines.

The flowers fade and are gone when the summer brightens the mountains. Then on 1 November, the date of John E. Cameron's death, the columbine bouquet appears again. Despite cold north winds and early snows, they are there. Placed at the grave by loving, unknown hands, have the flowers come out of the past like a song out of the wind?

In decades gone by a few people have seen a beautiful lady at the Cameron monument. She wore a dress of black satin brocade from the 1880s and in her hair were columbines and wild flowers. Observed sometimes on 5 April but most often on 1 November, the lady always placed a bouquet of blue columbines on John Cameron's grave, where she lingered lost in memories of a distant glorious day. Softly the evening shadows fell and softly the lady walked into the twilight mist. No one knew who she was. No one knew where she went. Like poetry and mystery she had come and gone. Like magic she had touched the forlorn grave with a spring song.

The years have tangled tall weeds among the stones of this quiet hill, and the names of those buried here seem all but forgotten; still, the lady brings her song, her secret, to John Cameron.

John E. Cameron was born 16 August 1859 in Carlton Place, Perth, Canada. He was the only child of Robert and Catherine Cameron, both Canadians and descendants of the Camerons of Locheil, Scotland. The following year the family moved to Wisconsin and later to Illinois and then to Nebraska. In 1866 they arrived in Black Hawk, Colorado, settling finally in Central City the following year when John was seven years old.

As an adult, John joined the Central City Rescue, Fire and Hose Company Number One. Having inherited his father's charm and his mother's gentleness and generosity, John was a favorite with his fellow firemen and was promoted to first assistant foreman in a short time. In 1886 he received an award of valor for his part in rescuing trapped miners from a cave-in. Children adored him, and society ladies could not resist him, inviting him to dinners and parties every chance they had.

Ladies with available young daughters especially invited the handsome, blue-eyed fireman to their houses, hoping their daughters would march him to the matrimonial rails. John managed to evade the hopeful lasses, much to their contriving mothers' surprise and regret. Gossips whispered that the young man's heart already belonged to someone special, but the anxious young ladies were hard put to discover the Someone's identity.

The gossips said the Someone was beautiful—she had to be, since they would never allow otherwise for *their* John Cameron. Since he was known to take long walks to Nevadaville or Bald Mountain, the gossips surmised the Someone lived there. It must have been one of them who put the cryptic notice in the *Daily Register Call:* "J. Cameron's lively interest in Bald Mountain might lead one to believe he is soon to renounce mossy bachelorhood." What a burr in the ladies' tails who had polished their daughters into bundles of irresistability. What a prattling of ground squirrels when these ladies decided to make one last assault on the gentleman (for their daughters, of course!) before he escaped for good. A barrage of party invitations were fired his way, but he always went in the company of his friends, Charles Franks, Richard Jenkins, and others, never with a lady.

Throughout the brilliant, flowered summer of 1887 John continued his strolls over the green hill to Bald Mountain and continued in the state of "mossy bachelorhood." Certainly the gossips, racked by curiosity, continued their gabbling. But when autumn came, the henyard fell silent, sadly silent and reflective.

John Edward Cameron died suddenly on Tuesday, 1 November 1887.

He was twenty-eight years old. Monday evening he had become ill, although it seemed to be nothing serious. The next evening while seated in one of the front windows of the family residence, he grew suddenly worse, calling out to his mother and collapsing dead at her feet. Although John was young and in good health, the doctor said he died of a "paralysis of the heart."

The following Sunday John was buried from the First Presbyterian Church. The funeral service was overcrowded, with people standing in the aisles and vestibule. Former Fire Chief Thomas Lucaas expressed his heartfelt admiration, saying, "John was a man loved by all, who cared for everyone he met."

The procession from the church to the Masonic Cemetery was befitting a prince, with the solemn glass-paneled, black-plumed hearse slowly driving up the hill, led by the Gilpin County Reed and Brass Band and followed by the fire departments of Black Hawk and Central, all the men in dress uniform. John was buried beside his father, who had died seven years earlier.

After the funeral, after the people had gone home, a young woman in mourning attire lingered by the new grave. Day after day she was noticed there, remaining many long hours. In the spring she brought wild roses and columbines and planted a small rosebush beside the tombstone. Then late in June she stopped coming.

Two years later, on the anniversary of John's death, the sexton reported seeing a young lady in black at the Cameron grave. A curious woman she was, as mysterious as the gray autumn clouds hanging over the hills. She placed spring flowers in the yellow grass of John's grave. The gossips had much speculation on this, especially since the sexton said the lady came from the direction of Bald Mountain. Yet no one in that city knew her. Anniversary followed upon anniversary, and the mysterious lady visited the Masonic Cemetery. Unnamed and impossible to get near, she also came one day each April, until the gossips concluded she was no lady at all: she was a ghost.

In 1899 a few rational people were disturbed to hear their fellow citizens call the "flesh and blood" lady at the Cameron monument a ghost. When these rational people observed her, they saw a living, breathing creature who walked up the hill as any living, breathing creature walked; she had been doing so for a dozen years now. At this time there was a handful of motley cynics who challenged a similar handful of motley spiritualists to prove once and for all that the mysterious lady was a ghost. After all, those who attributed ghostly qualities to her were a grave digger, a few worn-out miners, and the spiritualists, who saw ghosts in every cupboard. And what did Mrs. Cameron have to say?

Mrs. Cameron, who had opened her house to boarders since her son's death, was elusive on the subject. She had heard the tales of the woman, but had no intention of saying anything further to the motley handfuls. They agreed to hold a meeting at the grave.

On 1 November 1899, fourteen people gathered at the Masonic Cemetery. What the ratio of cynic to spiritualist was is impossible to discover, but at the end of the meeting there were no cynics left. In early evening, before sunset, the people were gathered behind each other at the gate when from the opposite side of the cemetery a beautiful lady was seen approaching the monument. She was dressed in mourning of a style ten years passed. The onlookers were speechless as they watched her place a bouquet of columbines on John's grave. She said something they were unable to understand.

Then one brave cynic among the group announced he was going to stop the lady. He started toward her. Without looking at him, she silently moved away in the direction from which she had come. The man ran after her, and a few of his fellows did likewise. The lady disappeared over the crest of the hill. When her pursuers reached that spot they saw no sign of her anywhere. At that moment a strong, sharp wind rose up, forcing the party to return to town. All the while the baffled, vexed cynics were saying, "There is no possible way we could have lost her. There is no possible place she might hide."

They never did solve the mystery of the lady. If Mrs. Cameron knew the truth, she kept it a secret until the day she died, 30 October 1912, at the age of eighty. Although she died in Denver, Catherine was buried on the quiet hill beside her husband and son.

The mysterious lady in black remained young and beautiful. No one ever described her otherwise. As decades passed she became more of a mystery, her identity lost forever. Many tales surrounded her, making it difficult to discern fact from fancy.

Of course the gossips had said from the beginning that the lady was John Cameron's only love. Stories said the two were to be married on 5 April, thus accounting for the lady's visits on that date. Some liked to add a bit of scarlet and intrigue, claiming John was poisoned by a jealous girl who decided that if she could not have him, no one would. After her deed was done, she killed herself and haunted his grave. Other tales had the beautiful lady refusing her suitor and John dying of a broken heart, after which the lady was driven by guilt. Still other stories said that no one could see the lady unless they believed in her; or one had to go to the grave at midnight with the requisite full moon shining. Who will ever know?

Who will ever understand the poetry of columbines and melancholy autumn wind? Who will ever know what great undying love was in John Cameron's heart? Who will ever know what sun-splashed memories of joy linger beside that column of marble?

CHAPTER XXI

Resurrection And Wrath

esurrection day dawned unexpectedly and without heavenly trumpets for the residents of Denver's City Cemetery in 1893. Nor was it seraphim who lifted the dead from their resting places. The hands of sweat-stained workmen jolted the departed into morning sunlight.

Graves were opened a row at a time, while a crowd of gawking curiosity seekers pressed around the workmen. Pried up with shovels or smashed in when stubborn, coffin lids were removed. The sacred dust and decaying bones of the dead were then spaded into boxes, numbered, and chucked on a wagon.

Workmen and some spectators pocketed a Bible here and a ring there. Without a whispered prayer, without respect, muted men and women were broken and cursed and robbed in death and tossed about like potatoes in a harvest field.

When the wagon was fully loaded with boxes and covered with a tarpaulin, the driver cracked his whip and went off, singing in a jolly voice, "Rattle their bones over the stones; they're only a pauper's, whom nobody owns; only a pauper's whom nobody owns."

Pauper's, true, these bones from gaping, defiled wounds in the earth. Murderers, thieves, and prostitutes, the penniless, nameless, wretched humanity had found their rest here at least. Though loathed in life, they became hallowed in death. Yet they were now disturbed from dreamless sleep.

Madam Cynara in her tangle of shawls cried a warning at the edge of the graves, "Go gently! Go gently! Whisper a prayer, or they will return. They will come!"

But the workmen jeered. Madam Cynara was no more than a potty eccentric old goose. She had ribbons flitting in her gray hair and surely in her gray brain. What was there to fear in those long dead? What was there to fear in the words of an old woman who collected rags and bits of paper and wax?

"A bone for you, Mrs. C?" called a workman.

"Go gently," she cried back, "or they will come!"

Scarcely had the wholesale exhumation begun the morning of 10 March 1893 when rumors spread around the neighborhood that ghostly forms were seen on the streets and in the nearby gardens. With work of this nature going on, the appropriate rumors were to be expected. Yet many citizens shuddered, observing City Cemetery from a respectful distance, believing there was more than rumor when men disturbed the dead, breaking their rest, awakening by thoughtless abuse these unknown paupers and wretched mortals.

Their shades flew into the angry air, a confusion of soft sounds and wrath, alighting lost in the day-bright world or fleeing into surrounding houses. They remained, hidden from night lanterns, caught between worlds. They remained, watching the passing of the seasons, bound to the place of their burial, when at last City Cemetery became Cheesman Park. They remain yet in the pavilioned, oak- and spruce-shadowed park, where their bones are fragmented and scattered beneath the broad green lawn, forgotten beneath unknowing feet.

The cemetery was established in 1858 by William Larimer about two miles from the young city of Denver. On a hill with a splendid view of the Front Range, the 320-acre site was called Mount Prospect. Many of Denver's pioneer citizens were interred here, their graves marked with elaborate marble or granite headstones, or simply a numbered wooden marker. A few graves were completely unmarked.

Mount Prospect, never a verdant garden due to lack of water, had deteriorated by the 1880s into a desolate, cactus-covered spot. Although the Hebrew and Catholic portions of the cemetery were well kept, the tract that was now called City Cemetery, bordered by Eighth and Thirteenth avenues, Race and Franklin streets, was derelict and saw few burials other than those at county and hospital expense. It was called "Pauper's Row," "Pauper's Hill," "Boothill," or sometimes "O'Neill's Ranch," after a murdered man who was buried there.

In 1887 newspapers were calling the cemetery "hideously ugly." "It is so ugly," wrote the *Denver Republican* 16 March, "that if there are any buried there with any sense of the artistic, or longings for the beautiful, they must turn over in their graves and groan at thought of what is above them."

Numerous unknown and unmonied citizens were buried in Pauper's Row without anything to mark the location of the grave. Sometimes several coffins were put in the same hole. While workmen were digging the ditch for the new water main in 1887, they accidentally struck one of these unmarked graves. The men felt uneasy. One who had been swearing turned away his face, remaining subdued the rest of the day.

Shortly thereafter, the idea of transforming City Cemetery into a park was circulated. The public happily approved. Since funds were needed for such an undertaking, Senator Henry Teller took the proposal to Washington, telling Congress the park would be honorably titled "Congress Park."

Meanwhile, in 1888 all the bodies in the Grand Army section of the cemetery were removed to Riverside Cemetery next to the Platte. The Masons, Odd Fellows, and private citizens also disinterred their beloved dead during the following four years, reburying them at Riverside or Fairmount. The removals were done with respect, gaining little attention from the public. The Catholic and Hebrew cemeteries were to be left undisturbed, since only the tract known as City Cemetery was then to become a park.

After legal disentanglements, petitions, discussions, and an appropriation of funds from the U.S. Congress, the project got under way. The city awarded E.P. McGovern, an undertaker, the contract for removing between 6,000 and 10,000 bodies from City Cemetery. His contract specified that each body was to be placed in a new box measuring twelve by forty-two inches.

Although a five- or six-foot corpse hardly fit gracefully into a forty-two inch box, McGovern was unperturbed. His crew of eighteen men casually broke up the bones and shoveled them with a bit of earth and a bit of old coffin wood into two or three boxes, then marked each as a single body and charged accordingly. It was an easy way to make a handsome profit on dead flesh. To fill 5000 boxes, McGovern had only to dig up 2500 graves.

John E. Wood, superintending the work for the health department, looked the other way. He made no noise over private profit nor over the violation of the dead. But the public and the press soon discovered the scandal. Observers also found that workmen and curiosity seekers were taking souvenirs from the graves and corpses.

Citizens became outraged that the dead were being desecrated, robbed, and broken. Graves were left open with fragments of bones yet in the dirt. One grave containing an iron coffin with the decomposing body of a bearded man peering through the broken lid was left open to view for two weeks before anyone removed it. There were rumors that at night men in the science profession spirited away a few of the better-preserved corpses.

On 17 March 1893, while a group of children and adults were watching the workmen remove a coffin from a grave, the coffin was dropped, and the decayed contents went sprawling out. The corpse was that of a young woman, her long damp locks ripe with mold. Her flesh was blackened and leathery. She had no eyes and her lips were drawn back in a ghastly grin.

The spectators moved away with a sound of murmuring as the workmen prepared to place the body in a box. Suddenly there was a moaning from the corpse, and the men, L.J. Hood and Dan Vogel, stepped back in fear. Hood laughed nervously, accusing his partner of making the noise.

"It's just in the mind," said Vogel with a shrug.

The corpse was broken and shoveled into two boxes. Immediately Vogel took a rest from the work, his hands visibly shaking. He glanced at the closed boxes, a sigh escaping him.

As word of the abominable work spread, the wrath of the public blazed. A fence was constructed around the job site, and the health department prohibited all spectators. But the wrath of the dead was yet to come.

"Go gently," cried Madam Cynara, "or they will return upon this place!"

And return they did.

Spirits, angered and lost, rose up and flew upon Jim Astor, one of the workmen who was acquiring a tidy collection of brass coffin plates engraved with brief epitaphs: "Gone to Rest," or "Blessed in Sleep," or "They Toil Not." Astor fled the work site one day after screaming in terror "No! No!" He flung the coffin plates on the ground as he ran away, nearly tumbling into a grave.

In the darkness of night a constant moaning was heard upon the hill. Residents in nearby homes were disturbed by the sounds night after night. Low, almost melodious, the moaning was like the wind yet unlike the wind. There was a quality of deep sadness in it, and something hideous and chilling.

Several residents in these surrounding houses encountered the dead of City Cemetery. The mistress of a house on Franklin Street saw spirit images in her mirrors. She never saw the forms within the rooms; only in the mirrors. Four distinct individuals, one a man with pistols slung on his hips, visited her in this fashion for many years. Houses in the area to this day are said to be haunted.

Some of the wretched, nameless wraiths fled into the shadows of gardens and there remained. Walking in the moonlight, their softly luminous forms twined trellis and arbor, fountain and summerhouse. At a house on Ninth Avenue, built in 1918, construction workers mentioned seeing a shadowy young woman watching nearby. Later this same figure, dressed in a plain frock, often visited the gardens of the house, singing a quaint song.

One night in 1894, Otto Carlson claimed to see two men who came down from the hill and passed into a house through the walls. Another man, Robert Teabury, encountered numerous hazy figures as he walked out of the Catholic cemetery one evening. The forms pressed close upon him, a whispering of emotion and darkness. Teabury said that for many days afterward he was ill.

When City Cemetery had finally become Congress Park, many of the deceased were left beneath the lawn. In 1907 the park's name was changed to honor the recently departed Walter S. Cheesman, a pioneer who had contributed much to Colorado. Time had closed the wounds of scandal, and the park was graced with a beautiful, white-columned pavilion in 1910, sacred to Cheesman's memory. Citizens forgot the silent dead, and many decades later the old Catholic cemetery was removed to Mount Olivet and the grounds made into the Boetcher Memorial Conservatory and Botanical Gardens.

But it is whispered that time has not put to rest the spirits of the desecrated dead. They wander wretched among the living in the park, seeking something they are unable to grasp. They are soft sound and quiet darkness, lingering among the marble columns at sunset, only shadowed air of twilight wind. Theirs is a deep longing and a deeper wrath.

Unnamed, unknown, unremembered, these dead make no footfalls as they drift hopelessly through arbored gardens, peering in at windows, passing in at stone walls. They are a cry in the rain, a tear in the grass, broken, rejected, lost in the mist between worlds.

CHAPTER XXII

Brimstone Marauders

he ponderous eyelids of Law had dropped, and the starched countenance of Order had been whisked away to some brick bed, leaving the silent courtrooms to John McAdow, his sloshing mop, and his sentimental tunes. Each night he and D.P. Demarest, the night watchman, were the only souls on the premises of the Denver Courthouse at Sixteenth and Tremont. At least they were the only souls with bodies still firmly in tow.

John McAdow spent each night polishing away any sign of judge and jury, attorney and clerk, defendant and plaintiff, telling himself he was a right lucky man to have the job and nothing would ever induce him to give it up. No indeed.

One chill November night in 1900 while McAdow was singing and humming snatches of a ballad, he rubbed out the last vestiges of a sloppy attorney and glanced up at a figure in the open doorway. He no sooner had said, "Evening, Mr. Demarest," than he realized no one was there.

"Funny—" began McAdow. He shrugged, drawing his mop across the floor.

"Evening, Mr. Dem—" said John McAdow, as he looked up a second time to see there was no one where he thought he saw someone.

Footfalls echoed out in the darkened corridor. McAdow grinned. Hurrying to the door, he leaned out with a loud, "Aha!" No one was there. He looked in the other direction. No one presented himself there either.

McAdow stood rubbing his chin. A ghastly scream disturbed his musing. Rushing down the hall in the direction of the sound, the janitor called out for the watchman, thinking some ill had befallen him. The watchman was out of sight and seemed to be out of earshot as well. Finally McAdow found him drinking coffee in his room on the third floor.

"Done heard that scream?" asked John McAdow breathlessly.

"No," was the reply.

"It was near the elevator on the second floor. And I done heard someone first arunning down the hallway."

"Could be someone broke in," said Demarest. "I'd better check the doors."

The doors, north, south, and west, declared themselves firmly bolted, and the ground floor windows were secure.

"Are you certain it was a scream?" said the watchman.

The reply was affirmative.

The two men searched each floor of the entire building, but found no intruder. After McAdow returned to his cleaning, D.P. Demarest continued walking about the courthouse quietly, checking and re-checking courtrooms, elevators, closets, and corridors. The only sounds he heard were his own footfalls and the low humming of the janitor.

The following night, Demarest was on the first floor when he heard screaming coming from above. No sooner had he reached the second floor than the screaming sounded from below. He returned to the first floor and saw the doors of the lift rattling furiously. A scream echoed down the hall. In a few moments McAdow ran to Demarest's side.

"What that be?" said the janitor, grabbing the watchman's arm. "I heard it in the basement."

Together the men descended the stairs slowly, with great caution. Demarest turned on the lights. All was silent in the depths save the burping of the boiler. Then they heard a groaning, as of a dying man, in the direction of the elevator. Demarest pulled the gate open and switched open doors. The noise ceased. For the remainder of the night the courthouse was at peace.

At one o'clock the next morning, John McAdow was sweeping one of the courtroom floors when he smelled sulfur. It became so strong that he hurried out of the room, choking. In the dim light of the corridor he saw two misty forms hurrying away from him. He cried out for the watchman.

"Ghosts! Ghosts!" yelled McAdow as D.P. Demarest came to his assistance. "Two. They gone down the hall. And brimstone. Smell it?"

Demarest nodded but said nothing. He stared into the gloom at the end of the corridor, unsure how to deal with ghosts. Does one beat ghosts with a stick? Shoot them? The watchman chose to turn on most of the courthouse lights, hoping excessive illumination would discourage the spooks.

Lit up like the Fourth of July in the dark hours before dawn, the courthouse came to the attention of city officials. No one could ignore the display. Demarest explained the next morning that he had been searching for possible trespassers. That pacified the booming officials until a judge and a few clerks complained of sulfurous odors in one of the courtrooms. There was no explanation Demarest could offer. Tell them he suspected ghosts and there would vanish his prized seventy-five-dollar-a-month job.

That night, as the twelve o'clock hour approached, Demarest went around the building switching on most of the lights. He could not abide another night in the gloom with a pair of brimstone spooks. He also had earlier covered the wall above his bed with a large American flag, convinced that the Stars and Stripes would keep the spirits out of his third-floor room, as sure as he was a citizen of the United States. Not that citizens had any special immunity to ghosts.

John McAdow likewise.desired protection from the spirits and had brought along his guitar. Not that guitar music had any special effect on ghosts.

Three o'clock in the morning approached with a brilliant courthouse occupied by a patriotic watchman and a guitar-strumming janitor. Both men thought certainly the lights, flag, and music would keep the night intruders at a distance.

If anything, however, these well-intentioned efforts increased the spirit population at the courthouse. Instead of a pair, a pack of spooks descended on John McAdow and D.P. Demarest.

When the clock struck three times, a scream echoed throughout the top floor. McAdow clutched his guitar closer, his brown eyes fixed on the watchman, waiting for a decision. Both men waited in silence, hoping the decision would present itself.

The terrible broken scream seemed to descend to the basement. A painful sound followed. Demarest mumbled that he had best check the basement.

Well lighted, the basement was silent when the two men reached it. They stood by the stairs for a moment, too frightened to make a sound, as a creeping sensation spread over them. A groaning rose from behind the elevator door. John McAdow gasped.

"Fred Swensen," he whispered. "Lawd save us!"

Demarest gave him a look of startled realization. Fred Swensen was an elevator pilot who had been killed the previous April by a fall down the shaft from the top floor to the basement.

Holding his breath and staring at the elevator, the watchman was considering telling the deceased Mr. Swensen exactly where he could get off when a hideous shriek resounded from the first floor. This latest noise was different and more chilling than any other. Demarest rushed up the stairs with McAdow close behind.

As the two entered the corridor, they saw several filmy forms flit down the hallway and pass into a courtroom. The men followed. They were greeted by the obnoxious perfume of brimstone and were forced to back out of the room immediately.

Demarest whispered his opinion to the janitor that the spirits perhaps belonged to some former defendants who had received unpleasant sentences and had come to wreak vengeance on the entire justice system.

Looking up and down the bright corridor, John McAdow began humming, "Swing Low, Sweet Chariot," hoping to call that eternal chariot to fetch the escaped spirits and return them to their proper habitat. Unfortunately, the chariot failed to arrive, but for an hour silence prevailed in the building. It was an uneasy silence, as the men tried to occupy themselves while glancing over their shoulders for the expected unexpected.

At four o'clock Demarest reluctantly ascended to the third floor to see if all was well. He walked slowly and close to the walls. He opened doors and quickly stood back. That floor proved spookless.

On the second floor the watchman felt the hair stand up on his neck. He strained to hear anything unusual. Suddenly he saw a misty figure pass out of one of the courtrooms. The scent of sulfur followed. Having lost any shreds of courage that might have been left in him, Demarest fled in the opposite direction. He nearly tripped down the flight of steps, only to see several spirits at the bottom. He turned on his heel and ran back upstairs.

The following day D.P. Demarest and John McAdow turned in their resignations, claiming ghosts as the reason and swearing they heard the dead Mr. Swensen's spirit. Demarest said he was going to Cripple Creek, exchanging his once comfortable room and salary—and those blooming spooks!—for the pleasantly precarious occupation of mining.

Although both men were eyed with suspicion, courthouse officials and clerks were not too hasty to pass judgment, for the building was pervaded by the unpleasant odor of sulfur. More than one clerk had looked over his shoulder when a creeping sensation came upon him.

Charles E. Estabrook succeeded Demarest, and Frank Heatly took the place of McAdow. Neither of these new men encountered the spirits, and soon the sulfur perfume, whatever its source, ceased to assail the courts.

The chariot, though late, had at last come for the brimstone spooks.

BIBLIOGRAPHY AND ACKNOWLEDGMENTS

Anderson, Joseph. Records. Colorado State Archives, Denver.

Baird, J.D. "First Gold Find in the Mountains," *The Trail*, Vol. xiv No. 9, 1922.

Bell, William A. *New Tracks in North America.* London: Chapman and Hall, 1869.

Bickman, William D. *From Ohio to the Rocky Mountains.* Dayton, Ohio: Journal Book and Job Printing House, 1879.

Binckley & Hartwell. *Southern Colorado: Historical and Descriptive of Fremont and Custer County,* 1879.

Blackmore, William. *Colorado: Its Resources and Prospects.* London: Ranken & Co., 1869.

Bowles, Samuel. *In the Parks and Mountains of Colorado.* Springfield, Mass: S. Bowles & Co., 1869.

Boyer, Henry. Private records. Denver Public Library, Western History Dept. (DPL WHD)

Brewer, William H. *Rocky Mountain Letters 1869.* (DPL WHD)

Brown, Dee. *Bury My Heart at Wounded Knee.* New York: Bantam Books, 1971.

Brown, John. *The Mediumistic Experience of John Brown, the Medium of the Rockies.* Des Moines: M. Hull & Co., 1887.

Brown, Robert L. *Ghost Towns of the Colorado Rockies.* Caldwell, Idaho: Caxton Printers, 1969.

Brown Silver Mining Company of Colorado. Philadelphia, 1868.

Buckman, George R. *Colorado Springs*. New York: Trow Print, 1893.

Canfield, John G. *Mines and Mining Men of Colorado*. Denver: Canfield, 1893.

Copeland, W.D. *One Man's Georgetown*. Privately printed. Georgetown Library.

Cushman, Samuel. *The Mines of Clear Creek County, Colo.* Denver: Times Steam Printing House, 1876.

Dilke, Sir Charles Wentworth. *Greater Britain, a record of travel in English-speaking countries, from New York to San Francisco*. New York: Harper & Bros., 1869.

El Paso County Coroner's inquest records.

Ferril, William C. Scrapbook. (DPL WHD)

Ferril, William C. *Sketches of Colorado*. Denver: The Western Press Bureau Co., 1911.

Field and Farm Magazine. Various articles, prior to 1918.

Fossett, Frank. *Colorado: Its Gold and Silver Mines*. New York: C.G. Crawford, 1880.

Freeman, J.W. *South Park and the Alpine Pass*. St. Louis: Woodward & Tiernan Co., 1896.

Frost, Aaron. *History of Clear Creek and Boulder Valleys, Colo.* Chicago: O.L. Baskin & Co., 1880.

Graham, Margaret Weber. Scrapbook, private papers.

Great Divide Magazine. Various articles, prior to 1900.

Griffin, H.M. Letters, private papers.

Hafen, LeRoy R. *Colorado and Its People*, 1948.

Hall, Frank. *History of the State of Colorado*. Chicago: The Blakely Printing Co., 1889 and 1895.

History of the Arkansas Valley, Colo. Chicago: O.L. Baskin & Co., 1881.

History of the City of Denver, Arapahoe County and Colo. Chicago: O.L. Baskin & Co., 1880.

Hill, Alice Polk. *Tales of the Colorado Pioneers.* Denver: Pierson & Gardner, 1884.

Hoig, Stan. *The Sand Creek Massacre.* Univ. of Oklahoma Press, 1961.

Ingersoll, Ernest. *Crest of the Continent.* Chicago: R.R. Donnelley & Sons, 1885.

Ives, James R. *Colorado State Business Directory.* Denver, 1884.

McGrath, Maria Davies. *The Real Pioneers of Colorado.* The Denver Museum, 1934.

Original Record of Buckskin Joe Mining District, 24 Sept. 1860 to 9 Oct. 1861. State Historical Society Library. (SHSL)

Randall, Jesse S. *Annals of Clear Creek County.* Unpub. (SHSL)

Randall, Jesse S. Scrapbooks and journals.

Smiley, Jerome C. *History of Denver.* Denver: Times-Sun Pub. Co., 1901.

Teetor, Henry Dudley. "Mines and Miners of Georgetown," *Magazine of Western History,* 12 Sept. 1890.

Thayer, William Makepeace. *Marvels of the New West.* Norwich, Conn.: Henry Bill Pub. Co., 1887.

Van Wagenen, Theodore Francis. *Notes on Colorado,* personal journal. (DPL WHD)

Vickers, W.B. *History of Clear Creek and Boulder Valleys.* Chicago: O.L. Baskin & Co., 1880.

Warren, Henry L. *Cripple Creek and Colorado Springs.* Warren and Stride, 1896.

Whitney, Ernest. *Legends of the Pike's Peak,* 1892.

Wright, E.S. Journal and private records. (DPL WHD)

Wolle, Muriel Sibell. *Stampede to Timberline.* Chicago: Sage Books, 1949.

NEWSPAPERS

Aspen Daily Times

Boulder Daily Camera

Boulder News and Courier

Canon City Record

Carbonate Chronicle (Leadville)

Central City Miners Register

Central City Register Call

Chaffee County Democrat

Chronicle-News (Trinidad)

Colorado Springs Gazette

Colorado Transcript (Golden)

Colorado Tribune (Denver)

Cripple Creek Crusher

Denver Post

Denver Republican

Denver Times

Elbert County Banner

Evening Chronicle (Leadville)

Fairplay Flume

Florence Daily Tribune

Fort Collins Courier

Georgetown Courier

Georgetown Miner

Glenwood Post

Idaho Springs News

Julesburg Advocate

Lake City Phonograph

La Plata Miner

Manitou Springs Journal

Meeker Herald

Mill Run (Montezuma)

Montezuma Journal (Cortez)

Park County Bulletin (Alma)

Pueblo Chieftain

Rocky Mountain Herald

Rocky Mountain News

Rosita Index

Saguache Cresent

San Miguel Examiner (Telluride)

Silver Cliff Prospector

Silver Cliff Rustler

Silver Cliff Silver Standard

Silver Plume Silver Standard

Silverton Standard

Solid Muldoon (Ouray)

Springfield Herald (Baca Co.)

Summit County Journal (Breckenridge)

Telluride Daily Journal

Telluride Journal

Trinidad Chronicle

Victor Daily Record

Wet Mountain Tribune

Many thanks to all the people across Colorado who have shared their ghost stories with me and who have contributed in some way to this book over the past eight years—I could never have gotten along without you! And a very special thanks to the following:

Mrs. Mary Ellen Barnes
Mr. Rudolph Barth
Mrs. Cynthia Carey
Mr. David Collins
Mr. Michael Daly
Mr. Lawrence J. Entz (Mayor of Silver Cliff)
Mr. Albert Fuentes
Mr. Pete Gones
Mrs. Bonnie Hardwick (DPL WHD)
Mr. Oscar Malek
Mrs. Violet Griffin Richards
Mr. George Rowe
Mr. & Mrs. Joe Schaffer
Mr. Darrel Solomon (Clear Creek Co. Archivist)
Mr. J.A. Vandermeer
Mr. David Williams
Mr. Jim R. Wright

And the people of:

Colorado State Historical Society Library
Denver Public Library, Western History Dept.
Pioneer Museum, Colorado Springs
Fremont & Custer Co. Historical Society
Leadville Historical Association
Ouray County Historical Society
San Juan County Historical Society
San Miguel County Historical Society

GOD BLESS THEM ALL!!!